Processing
The Adventure
Experience

Reldan S. Nadler, Psy. D.
John L. Luckner, Ed.D.
Adventure Consultation & Therapy (ACT)
Santa Barbara, CA

KENDALL/HUNT PUBLISHING COMPANY
2460 Kerper Boulevard   P.O. Box 539   Dubuque, Iowa 52004-0539

Contents

Preface

This book is a compilation of the authors' experiences, both as instructors and consultants in adventure-based programs. In recognition of the growing interest and popularity in the field and the essential role that processing plays in designing and delivering quality experiences, this book addresses the need to integrate state-of-the-art counseling theory and adventure-based programming practices. Applied psychological theory and effective educational practices are synthesized for the reader. A theory of change is presented along with strategies and techniques to be used in the field. This book is designed to be used as a resource for leaders, educators, trainers, and therapists who employ adventure-based activities and ropes course events in educational settings, mental health programs, corporate consultation and training, and inpatient and outpatient chemical dependency programs.

Both beginning and seasoned instructors will find valuable information that can be used to help process adventure experiences and facilitate generalization and transfer. This book can be used in parts to learn a specific skill or activity, such as strategies for developing and using metaphors, or it can be read from cover to cover in an effort to build or expand your current knowledge and skills base.

This book is not meant to replace acquiring sound group processing and counseling skills. We caution readers to use only the techniques and strategies that are within their scope of competency, training, and comfort. This ensures that both the instructors and the students will have a quality experience.

It is our sincere hope that the field of adventure-based programming will continue to proliferate in scope and quality of services provided. In addition, we hope that you, as a professional in the field will continue to challenge yourself to pursue opportunities for positive personal and professional growth. Finally, we hope that you find this book to be a valuable resource that will help you create new opportunities for significant learning and breakthroughs for your students.

Acknowledgments

We would like to thank the many persons who have assisted us in the completion of this text. Relly would like to acknowledge his wife, Juli, for her continual support, love and encouragement. His family, Ann, Martin, Patricia, Nancy, Larry, and Ivan for their inspiration and faith in him. John would like to thank his wife, Sue, for her caring and giving nature as well as for sharing her expertise in this area. Also, he appreciates all his outdoor-adventure friends who help make the living-learning process so much fun. Finally, we both would like to acknowledge the members of the Association of Experiential Education for their support at our seminars and the honest feedback about what they want and need to facilitate better adventure-based courses.

Introduction

It is the first day of your two-week adventure-based course. As the instructor, you have been planning this course for the past two days. You and your co-instructor have met and discussed your teaching styles and identified your personal strengths and some specific areas that you're striving to improve. You have made a course plan and written out the objectives that you would like to see this specific group of students attain by the end of the course. In addition, you have gone over their medicals, packed out the food and equipment, and have identified your needs for support and transportation. In general everything during course planning has gone quite smoothly. You're feeling good and prepared for this course.

The students were supposed to arrive about an hour ago but, because of transportation problems, it doesn't sound like they will be getting to the program site for another hour or two. This sets your plans back a bit, since you had an action-packed first day planned for them. When they finally arrive, two and a half hours late, you hustle through unpacking their suitcases. You help them sort their trail clothes from their street clothes and encourage them to leave all their extraneous clothes and accessories such as hair dryers, hunting knives and personal stereos behind.

With evening fast approaching, you decide that you have just enough time to do a group trust fall. The group walks over to an area that can be used for the activity and everyone becomes extremely involved in it. All of the members of the group finish without a minute of sunlight left to spare. One group member, Mary, is very fearful and tentative, while another, Bob, is loud and condescending to the others. The group needs to set up their tents and make dinner in the dark, which you figure is a good experience for them since they are all excited from the trust fall and first-day enthusiasm. You and your co-instructor help the group set up camp and also show them how to use the stoves since many of them probably have never cooked on a stove before.

Dinner and casual conversation go well. There are many questions that people are asking about what to expect for the next 14 days. You avoid answering as many of these questions as possible because you want them to be in the here and now rather than to be worrying about what is going to happen days from now. One female, Betsy, you notice is sitting by herself and hasn't said a word to anyone. By the time everyone has cleaned up and put everything away, you see that their energy is beginning to dwindle. Though you had planned to have a group discussion about goals and expectations, you sense that it wouldn't be well received at this time of night and decide to do that tomorrow.

When you wake up the next morning, it is pouring rain and everyone including yourself is reluctant to get out of their nice dry sleeping bag and tent. But you manage to drag yourself out, put some water on the stoves and shake the tents. Needless to say everyone is sluggish and slow to rise, but in due time they come together for hot drinks and breakfast. One person, Jim, begins to grumble about the weather and question whether he can "hack it." You and your co-instructor spend some time planning the day while everyone is cleaning up.

After deliberating, you decide that you better put the discussion of goals and expectations on hold due to the weather and slow start. In addition, you need to begin hiking in order to get to the climbing site in two days time. Besides, you expect that the weather will clear by lunch and you have identified the location of a nice overlook where you can stop to eat and have a group talk.

Before we continue with our story of delayed group discussions, let's take some time to identify why they have not materialized. Looking back at what has occurred so far, what clearly comes across as the primary focus of this course? If you said "the activities," then we have conveyed the type of picture that we wanted.

Yes, when choices had to be made, the option of doing an activity was always chosen. Again looking back at what has happened so far within our scenario, can you pick out the junctures at which these choices were made and how options for bringing the group together for interpersonal interaction and personal expectations could have been derived?

Some opportunities for group cohesion and individual learning have been delayed, if not lost. What is it about trusting others that was hard for Mary? What are you going to do with Bob putting down others in the group? How can you help Betsy feel more comfortable about the course and interacting with others? What is going on with Jim and how do you prevent him from being your first dropout?

Some suggestions that you as the instructor could have used are to (a) have set the tents and tarps up when you found out that the bus was going to be late, (b) have each student identify and tell a feeling that they experienced right after the trust fall to set a tone, (c) have one instructor cook dinner while the other leads the group discussion, (d) have each student write one fear or apprehension about the course on a piece of paper without signing it. Mix the papers up and pass them out to be read aloud and discussed, (e) spend some individual time getting acquainted and building rapport with each of the students whose behaviors you noted earlier, (f) not doing the trust fall, (g) getting up an hour earlier, or (h) not breaking camp until you have spent time talking about the course.

At this point we would like to present the foundation and impetus for writing this text. We suggest that processing is an essential component of every adventure-based experience. Planning time for processing and appropriately structuring those sessions provides the greatest opportunity for the experience to have long-term personal effects. To be a successful facilitator of processing the experience, you will want to be able to integrate theoretical constructs of adventure-based learning with specific group process skills and techniques in order to enhance and cement the learning for students. Some of the contents that you'll find in this text include information on how to structure the group, leadership interventions, levels of processing, how to deal with repeated patterns of behavior, what to do with the expression of intense emotions, how to include reluctant students, and several examples of processing exercises.

Figure 1. Facilitating the Adventure-Based Experience

What Is Processing?

Processing is an activity that is used to encourage individuals to reflect, describe, analyze, and *communicate* what they have recently experienced (Quinsland & Van Ginkel, 1984). It is the cornerstone of an effective adventure-based learning experience. This point becomes evident when we take the time to examine experiential learning models.

While experiential learning models vary from theorist to theorist (i.e., Dewey, 1938; Kolb, 1984), it is generally agreed that optimally there are four distinct phases that comprise the learning cycle: experience, reflection, processing, applying, and back to experience (See Figure 2). Experience occurs naturally in all life situations. However, in educational or therapeutic situations, specific experiences need to be planned and implemented. The structured experience sets the stage for learning. This initial step can be viewed as the data-generating part of the experience. The second stage of the cycle entails setting aside some time for individuals to look back and examine what they saw, felt, and thought about during the event. The third stage is that of processing. After individuals have experienced an activity and reflected upon it, this is a time to share what

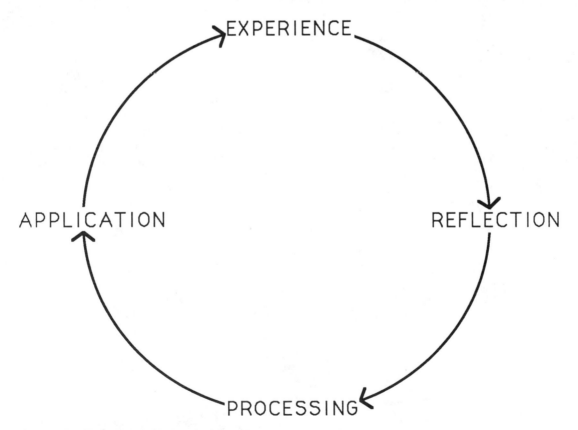

Figure 2. Experiential Learning Cycle

1

they saw, thought, and how they felt during the event. The intent here is to assist individuals to find out what happened at a cognitive, effective, and behavioral level—before the activity, while the activity was progressing, and after its completion. It is during this stage that individuals examine patterns of thoughts, feelings, and/or behaviors that occurred and try to make links with similar occurrences in other settings. They evaluate those patterns with respect to their value for personal and professional effectiveness. In addition, they consider ways to modify and enhance those particular aspects with regard to how they want to function in the future.

The last part of the experiential learning cycle is an essential stage. In essence, it is the primary reason that we spend time reflecting and processing. At this point, we focus on the central question "Now what?" Individuals apply what they have learned during this experience to actual situations in which they are involved in on the course, or at home, school, or work. It is a time to make specific plans for experimenting with different ways of thinking, feeling, and behaving. The completion of these four steps brings us back to the beginning of the learning cycle which is then initiated by the next experience.

Why Process?

The primary reason for processing is that adventure-based learning experiences are rich in symbols, metaphors, feelings, and typical behavior patterns. These patterns may continue to exist at an unconscious level whether or not one takes time to reflect and articulate them. The Greek philosopher, Socrates, has been quoted as saying, "Show me a man on an athletic field for one hour and I'll tell you more about him than if I had talked with him for eight hours."

Through experiential activities, you, as the leader, see and learn a great deal about course participants. Often, you notice patterns of behavior and interaction that neither the individuals themselves or their families are aware of. As a result, the challenge becomes how to help participants become aware of their thoughts, feelings and behavior patterns and how to transfer this new learning back to their home, work, or school setting.

Transfer and generalization occur when the learning in one situation carries over to another. An individual's *real* gain in a course should be measured by how much has been learned and if it can be sustained and applied after the experience. Therefore, it is our responsibility as leaders to do all within our power to increase this transfer of learning.

Much of the generalization and application can take place at the unconscious level. However, you can bring even greater success to your program by looking at some ways to increase the conscious aspects of the transfer of learning. This depends on several factors. First, participants must see the similarities between situations that happen on the course and situations in other aspects of life (e.g., resolving conflict verbally rather than stomping out or stuffing feelings). Second, individuals who see that new responses bring about beneficial results are more likely to be motivated to use this new learning (e.g., talking about fear, asking for support, sharing feelings). Third, it is helpful if participants see opportunities to use the new knowledge. This is encouraged by realistically comparing an adventure experience with specific past and possible future situations in their lives.

Participants involved in an adventure-based activity are engulfed and at times overwhelmed with new stimuli. There are new activities, intense emotions, new environments, and new personal relationships. Frequently, the experience engenders in participants feelings of fear, anxiety, exhilaration, exhaustion, peaceful solitude, camaraderie, pain, anger, alienation, sadness, frustration, and joy. Most of these feelings are experienced in a clearer, more intense manner than they are at home or work. The uniqueness of these feelings and experiences allow the group members to see themselves and their potentials differently. The physical, mental, emotional, spiritual, and environmental awareness are magnified. New learning and growth-producing experiences are potential results. The more participants digest, synthesize, and assimilate what's happening to them, the more self-knowledge that is available for change.

Processing teases out the richness of the experience so it stands out and apart, like the important lines of a page underlined with a yellow highlighter. These unique learnings can then be used again and generalized to other settings. When a new experience is processed, integrated, and internalized, it then can become a new chapter in students'

Figure 3. Traveling in New Environments

stories. This new reading of themselves allows students to stretch and grow into uncharted territory.

Processing is a developmental endeavor of discovering patterns and unique outcomes of course participants. It is a liberating and generating process that helps students construct a new reality or make up new meanings from their experiences. The end result allows individuals to have more choices in their lives.

To begin with, experiential approaches seek to educate the whole person—that is attention to the cognitive, affective and psychomotor domains. All feelings influence the mind, and in return the mind influences feelings. Thinking and feeling then are inextricably interrelated. Your challenge is to help participants become aware of this interrelationship and interdependency. Course activities afford members an opportunity to learn about themselves. The experiences are mirrors for how individuals respond when emotions are aroused. In psychological terms, participants "project" their personality and behavior patterns onto the experience. The results can be more graphic than what's seen in psychological testing with instruments such as the Rorschach ink blot test or the Thematic Apperception Test, where individuals make up stories about what's going on in a picture. Processing allows participants to own their projections.

Adventure-based activities are usually unfamiliar and elicit participants' true feelings, thoughts, and behavior patterns. The more unfamiliar and unexpected activities, the more projection of true self will follow. This process transpires unconsciously without the participants' intent. An example of this process is when participants are feeling afraid and fearful about the height of the ropes course. They think that they may get hurt or make a fool of themselves. The complementary action or behavior is to stay in the background and watch others until they feel they can get it right. A similar pattern may arise when individuals have a big project due at work. They feel they might get hurt, criticized, or embarrassed by doing it. Their complementary action then is to ask

ADVENTURE-BASED EXPERIENCE (A-B)   HOME AND WORK EXPERIENCES (H)

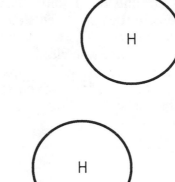

Awareness
Patterns of Behavior
Feelings
Conversations
Physiology
Beliefs
Defenses

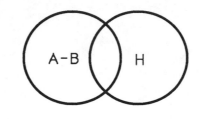

Responsibility
Owning Projections
Identifying Strengths
  & Typical Patterns
Blending Styles w/ Others
Surrender/Acceptance of
  Feelings & Roles
Parallel and Symbolic Nature
  of the Experience
Owning Self-Limiting Beliefs

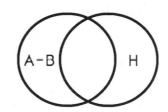

Experimentation
Increase Options
Risk Taking
Making Contracts
Asking for Feedback & Support
Reevaluation/Assessment

Generalization and Transfer
Carrying and Integrating the
  Experience
Making Choices and Changes
Commitment
Learning and Growth
Catalyst for Further
  Growth and Development

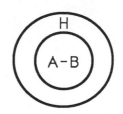

Figure 4. Processing for Generalization and Transfer

for more time or procrastinate until they get it right. The more participants understand their feelings of fear and embarrassment and their patterns to avoid it, the better chance they have of administering some change in similar fear situations at work, school, and at home. The activities and events may be different, but the emotions, thoughts, and behavior patterns are not. The following figure attempts to illustrate the manner in which thoughts, feelings, and behaviors that occur on an adventure-based course likely exist in one's home setting. Processing helps individuals bring the circles closer together and optimally they become interwoven so that growth in the adventure-based setting produces gains in the home, school, and work setting.

Adventure-Based Learning Process

In general, adventure-based learning is a type of educational and/or therapeutic program in which adventure pursuits that are physically and/or psychologically demanding are used within a framework of safety and skills development to promote interpersonal and intrapersonal growth (Bagby & Chavarria, 1980). Currently, there is a wealth of literature and research that substantiates the positive effect of using adventure-based programming with many diverse age groups and populations (e.g., Colan, 1986; Ewert, 1989; Rudolph, 1991). Drawing from the work of Walsh and Golins (1976), Piaget (1977), and Yalom (1975) we have attempted to develop a theoretical foundation that explains why adventure-based programs are effective. We suggest that by having a solid theoretical understanding of why adventure-based learning works and what the components of a successful course are, you can plan courses and make mid-course decisions that will enable both you and your students to experience positive gains from your time together. In addition, we suggest that while this model generally focuses on programs that are conducted in outdoor settings, individuals who conduct challenge programs indoors can enhance the quality of their courses by having an understanding of this model.

The following is a brief explanation of each of the components. They are graphically depicted in Figure 5.

1. **The Student:** Students come to the course with a preconception of what the experience is going to be like. Generally, the expectations that they have set the stage for a meaningful learning opportunity. For some students the anticipation causes a sense of internal stimulation. Other students do not experience this feeling until they are immersed in the course. This internal state that permits learning to occur is referred to as. . . .

2. **Disequilibrium:** Disequilibrium refers to an individual's awareness that a mismatch exists between old ways of thinking and new information. It is a state of internal conflict that provides motivation for an individual to make personal changes. Disequilibrium must be present for learning to occur. By involvement in an experience that is beyond one's comfort zone, individuals are forced to integrate new knowledge or reshape existent perceptions. These qualitative and quantitative changes are referred to as the processes of accommodation and assimilation. Students experience the state of disequilibrium by being placed in a. . . .

3. **Novel Setting:** Placement in an environment that one is not familiar with helps to breakdown individual barriers. When this factor is combined with the immersion into a group of virtual strangers, a heightened level of arousal develops. The underlying conditions of effort, trust, a constructive level of anxiety, a sense of the unknown and a perception of risk are integrated within a. . . .

7

4. **Cooperative Environment:** Establishing an atmosphere and method of teaching that makes use of cooperative rather than competitive learning fosters opportunities for students to develop group cohesiveness. This bonding is cultivated through a structure that focuses on shared goals and the provision of time for interpersonal and intrapersonal communication. This foundation exists while each individual and the group continually are presented with. . . .

5. **Unique Problem-Solving Situations:** New skills and problem solving situations are introduced to students in a sequence of increasing difficulty. The learning opportunities are concrete and can be solved when group members draw on their mental, emotional and physical resources. Completion of such tasks leads to. . . .

6. **Feelings of Accomplishment:** Success can lead to increased self-esteem, an increased internal locus of control, improved communication skills and more effective problem-solving skills. The meaningfulness of these success experiences is augmented by. . . .

7. **Processing the Experience:** Students are encouraged to reflect and in some manner express the thoughts and feelings that they are experiencing. Processing is essential if there is going to be. . . .

8. **Generalization and Transfer:** The ultimate goal of the adventure-based experience is to assist students in providing their own linkages, bridges, and connections to what they are learning so that they can integrate their personal insights and desired behaviors into their lifestyle during the remainder of the course and when they return home.

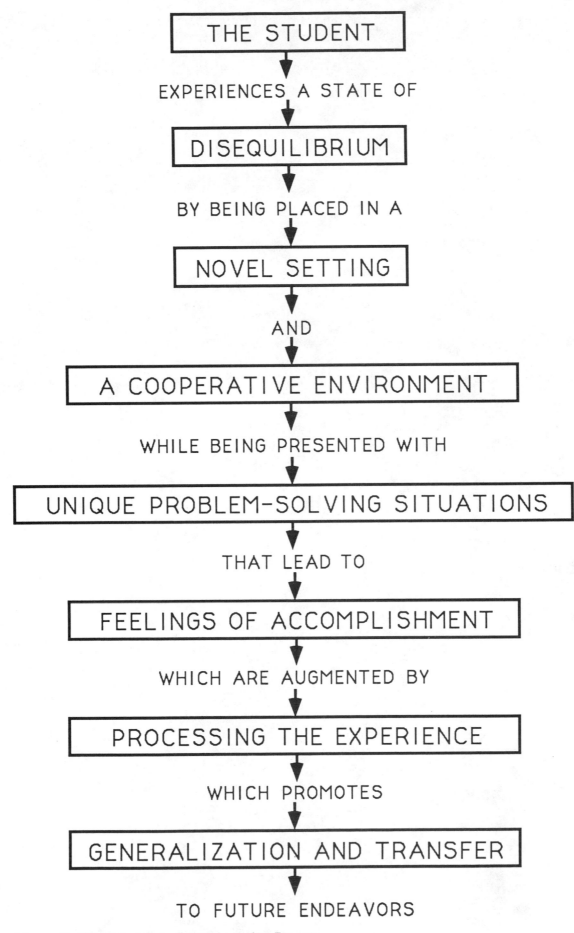

THE STUDENT

EXPERIENCES A STATE OF

DISEQUILIBRIUM

BY BEING PLACED IN A

NOVEL SETTING

AND

A COOPERATIVE ENVIRONMENT

WHILE BEING PRESENTED WITH

UNIQUE PROBLEM-SOLVING SITUATIONS

THAT LEAD TO

FEELINGS OF ACCOMPLISHMENT

WHICH ARE AUGMENTED BY

PROCESSING THE EXPERIENCE

WHICH PROMOTES

GENERALIZATION AND TRANSFER

TO FUTURE ENDEAVORS

Figure 5. The Adventure-Based Learning Process

Change Conditions

So how do people change? Why is adventure-based programming such a powerful change agent? Primarily, the answers to these questions lie in understanding the role of the state of disequilibrium as described earlier. The state of disequilibrium creates an unorganized affect or ego confusion wherein a quality of disorganization or dissonance predominates. The act of restructuring or reordering to regain balance (called equilibration) is where change in feelings, thoughts, attitudes, and behavior patterns occur. So it is in the process of getting lost, feeling anxious and uncomfortable, that individuals find their way and themselves. The process of change and conditions that enhance the state of disequilibrium are described below.

Defenses

Carl Whitaker (1981) described anxiety as the most primitive form of affect or feeling. People learn to develop defense mechanisms as an intrapersonal protection against their own anxiety. Some common defenses are denial, blaming others, taking control, anger, aggressiveness, being super responsible, perfectionism, intellectualizing, charming others, and humor. These defenses protect individuals from feeling some of their deeper feelings, such as, fear, inadequacy, loneliness, hurt, rejection, embarrassment, and helplessness. Figure 6, which has been adapted from Wegscheider (1979), attempts to show how we protect those core feelings with specific defensive behaviors.

When the wall of defenses can be shaken, even momentarily, some deep feelings might be experienced and accepted. The emotional arousal may be very intense. Without the normal defenses intact, disequilibrium becomes a driving force to attenuate the emotional intensity. At these times new ways of reacting and feeling can be tried. Individuals can get in touch with their feelings and deal with them constructively.

An adventure-based experience that includes each of the following change conditions promotes disequilibrium by taking away normal defense mechanisms. This process of disarmament forces people to search for new ways of relating, and provides the foundation for having a meaningful experience.

Change Conditions

These are conditions or states that people can be placed in to accentuate disequilibrium, dissonance, disorder, frustration, or anxiety. Enhancing these feelings increases the need to order, restructure, or alter one's cognitive map of the world and of oneself in an effort to restore equilibrium. Ilya Prigogine (1984) calls this restructuring "order out of chaos." Each of these conditions may be overlapping or interdependent.

11

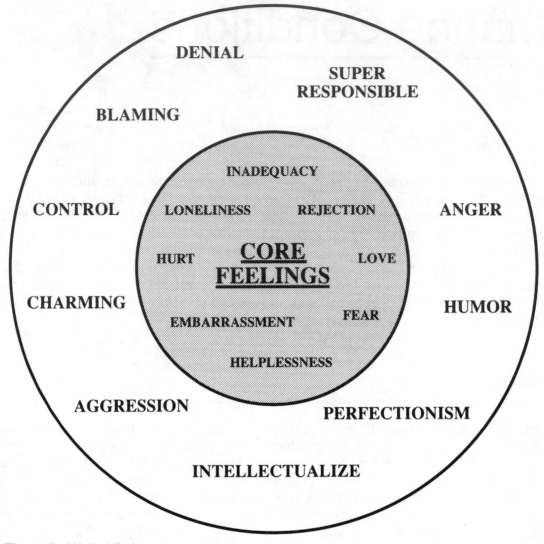

Figure 6. Wall of Defense

Understanding these conditions and finding ways to create them can increase your ability to promote change.

1. *Hope*—This condition exists when individuals view the experience as a way to dissolve some of their problems, heal their wounds, or fulfill their needs. There is an expectation of a positive outcome or attainment of a new goal. You can enhance course participants' sense of hope by: (a) telling stories about what other people took away from the experience in the past; (b) asking participants to write down and share their goals; (c) talking about their goals and how there is potential to attain them, and (d) helping participants break down their goals into smaller achievable steps so that they can reach their desired goals.

2. *Effort*—This condition entails taking physical, emotional, mental, and behavioral action. Risk-taking is encouraged. Every time one domain is activated, whether it is the cognitive, affective, or psychomotor, the other domains also become aroused. For example, the literature on running suggests that physical exercise also activates the emotions. In essence, there is a holistic connection that exists within our bodies.

Attention, concentration, and focusing are also aspects of effort. Another aspect of effort is surrender. It may take a lot of emotional effort to surrender to something, such as the situation or one's feelings. There are times that encouraging a surrender or giving up an unproductive pattern will entail a great deal of effort in order to beget a meaningful experience. Effort can be depicted by the cliches ''Go for it!'' or ''You only know how far you can go by going too far.''

Most adventure-based activities require physical, mental, and emotional effort. Additional ways that you can improve effort are by (a) encouraging all participants to talk and share their thoughts and feelings, (b) appointing leaders or recorders for the day, (c) asking participants to experiment with new roles or behaviors, and (d) pushing through resistance when people want to stop or quit.

3. *Trust*—This condition connotes an assured reliance or confident dependence on others, one's self, the leader, or the experience. The more trust that exists, the easier it is to make an effort or endure the tension of being in disequilibrium. Learning to trust one's own abilities and the resulting increase in self-esteem is a fundamental outcome of experiential education. On pages 209–215 of the activities section, there is information on how to develop and enhance feelings of trust.

4. *Constructive Level of Anxiety*—This condition exists when individuals feel in trouble, ambivalence, confusion, dissonance, discomfort, frustration, or stress. You want to continue to assess the group and each individual to ensure that the anxiety level is constructive and safe. Humans feel vulnerable when there is anxiety. When this disorientation occurs, it is possible that something meaningful can seep in when the defense system is less intact. In the psychological literature many authors call this change condition different things. Alfred Bandura called it ''emotional arousal''; Fritz Perls called it ''frustration''; and Ilya Prigogine called it ''chaos or fluxuations.'' To change, old structures have to be dissipated and new structures built in their place. Anxiety causes people to get out of the comfort zone, and try new behaviors to lessen the anxiety. You can enhance the constructive level of anxiety by (a) using handicaps (discussed on pages 158 to 162), (b) increasing the sense of the unknown, (c) increasing the perceptions of risk, (d) having participants experiment with new roles, and (e) doing activities differently, such as, in the dark or in novel ways.

5. *A Sense of the Unknown or Unpredictable*—This condition exists when individuals have a sense of awe or mystery regarding what they're going to experience. There's a limited time for rationalizing, defending, psyching up or psyching out. Participants ask many questions when experiencing this ambiguity. When possible answers should not be given, rather participants should be encouraged to experience and accept their feelings of uncertainty. Human brains are wired to develop structures or make meaning. The more unknown, unfamiliar, and unpredictable the experience, the harder people work to make sense of what is happening to them. The unpredictable keeps people off balance. They don't know what to set up barriers for and as a result they may experience something purely and naively. This sense of the unpredictable or unexpected compels individuals to live in the here and now.

The motivation to predict and control our environment and our behavior is very powerful and it's the reason the field of psychology began. When appropriate, you can harness this powerful change condition by (a) refraining from giving answers which let participants predict and control the future, (b) taking away watches from people if it is possible, (c) constantly changing rules or procedures so that partici-

Figure 7. Working Together on the Mohawk Walk

pants live in the unexpected, (e) using handicaps, (f) increasing the constructive level of anxiety, and (g) enhancing the perception of risk.

6. **Perception of Risk**—This condition exists when individuals perceive the experience as a physical, emotional, and behavioral risk or danger. It usually is a perceived risk in a student may say something like "I feel I may die or get hurt." In adventure-based programs there is a large contrast between the perceived risk and actual risk. One of the major components of processing is to help participants understand how their perceived risks are created and then transfer that learning to other perceived risks that exist in their lives.

Thompson (1981) stated, "Reactions to potentially stressful events depend on their meaning for the individual." She encourages people to assign meaning that will be most beneficial. You have many opportunities to use your processing skills to help participants integrate the learning and take responsibility for their perceptions. The perception of risk is engendered mostly by the activities. You can add to the perception of risk by (a) increasing the constructive level of anxiety, (b) increasing the sense of unknown and unpredictable by doing what is unexpected, and (c) developing behavior contracts for emotional and behavioral risks taken.

In summary, we have attempted to explain why people have meaningful experiences through participation on adventure-based courses. We suggest that the more you can enhance the six therapeutic change conditions to create disequilibrium, the less individuals are able to use their defenses to arrest the growth process. Therefore, in an attempt to restore equilibrium, participants reorder and restructure their cognitive, affective and behavioral maps. Consequently, they may be able to experience their core feelings in greater depth and come to feel better about themselves and the world that they live in.

General Guidelines for Working with Groups

As an adventure-based leader you continually will need to juggle many things in your mind in order to orchestrate quality courses. The following list of thoughts, goals, and considerations for facilitating a group has been adapted from Ebbe (1985) and the *Voyageur Outward Bound Instructor Handbook* (1988). They are presented in the spirit of helping you maintain focus on how to get the most out of each debriefing opportunity so that every group that you work with has a positive meaningful experience.

1. Try to suspend judgment and refrain from assuming someone's motives. Being non-judgmental and sensitive to someone else's point of view entails believing that all people are of equal worth, and all values and lifestyles are equally valid.

2. In your introduction let individuals know what to expect. Their pre-conceived expectations often create a barrier to learning from the unexpected.

3. Be clear about your role as a leader: to ensure safety, instruct, facilitate, observe, raise issues, and clarify. Simultaneously you need to be clear about what it is not: to force people to change, to judge them, and to lay your own values on them.

4. Be clear about where a group can have input and make choices, and what you will not change about the course. When giving the group a choice, spell out any parameters which they need to consider in their decision making, and be prepared to live with the choice they make.

5. Timing and pacing are essential. Reassess goals, individuals' needs, and group needs regularly.

6. Help individuals turn negative feelings into positive learning experiences. Remember disequilibrium is the catalyst for growth.

7. You can only take others as far as you have gone. The more in touch you are with your own feelings, patterns of communication and methods of resolving conflict, the easier it will be to facilitate learning in a group setting.

8. You can't expect to relate to the life experiences and problems of all individuals whom you work with. Be honest. Don't pretend to have answers you don't have. Ask good questions. Often group members can use each other as resources, and usually people can find their own answers, especially when encouraged to listen to their own inner wisdom. We can point out behavior and offer options as to ways to handle a situation, but individuals need to make their own decisions.

9. When honesty and respect are demonstrated and trust ensues, honest confrontations and open questioning are usually met with appreciation. Realize that for many people it takes a lot of courage to let down defenses and engage in open honest communication. We need to respect people for who they are. Some will disclose and share deeply; with others, what appears to be superficial and non-risky to us may be a large emotional risk to them.

10. The more you talk, the more silence from groups members will likely follow. If you are able to create an environment that is safe and on task, people will fill it with their thoughts and feelings.

11. Setting up a one-on-one norm (you talking to one member at a time) can stifle group interaction.

12. If an activity or method doesn't work, keep on moving and try something else.

13. Try not to overfocus or get into unsolvable problems.

14. If an individual is opening up and really helping the group, don't let the person dry up. Open up the group to all, widen the focus, and tie each person's issues into other's in the group. For example, you might say "Greg, we all know how Judy deals with her anger, how do you deal with yours?"

15. Look for common themes or issues in the group to link them to each other. Your job is similar to a weaver or tailor by connecting issues and people with each other and then continually drawing them in closer.

16. Ask members in the group what is it they want right now. Once it is made explicit, have the member ask others in the group directly for it—"Steve, can you support me when I'm scared? Jill, will you support me?" The more members can ask each other directly and assertively about what they want, the easier it is to transfer this learning to others outside the group. The group serves as a microcosm of the outside world.

17. While listening, look around to see how others are behaving and reacting.

18. If members begin to cry, you can still ask them questions or ask them to stop and pull themselves together.

19. Most people may not be ready to deal with an issue the first time it is brought up. If it's important, it'll come up again.

20. When there is intensity and strong emotions expressed at a group session, the next one is apt to be more superficial.

21. A group many times reflects the problems or dynamics of its leader.

22. The things that you choose not to say are many times the most accurate and facilitative. Learn to trust yourself and your intuition.

Group Ground Rules

When working with groups, it's important to lay the groundwork for the group process procedures. This structure helps participants feel safe and knowledgeable about what to expect. Some ground rules that you may want to consider are as follows:

1. The group should sit in a circle where everyone can see each other.

2. Ask participants not to lie down. Try to keep the energy of the group within the circle.

3. Introduce the group process. Some specifics that you may want to include are (a) speak honestly and openly with others, (b) this is a safe environment to explore feelings and learning from the experience, (c) listen and receive constructive feedback from others.

4. What is spoken in the group will remain confidential among the group members, unless the individuals give their permission to share their situation and feelings with others outside the group.

5. There is to be no physical violence in the group.

6. One person speaks at a time without interrupting others. Each person should listen and try to tune into what others are saying.

7. Everyone in the group belongs in the group. Only the leader can change this rule. If the group is unhappy with one person, this does not change the individual's membership in the group. The unhappiness is what needs to be worked through.

8. Everyone is ultimately responsible for his or her own behavior. No one should be forced into anything. Sometimes members need encouragement to try new things, but whenever possible they should have the right to say no or pass.

9. What is true for individuals must be determined for themselves. People may have different perceptions about an event that they have shared with others. As a result, peoples' emotions belong to them and should be considered true for that person.

Group Developmental Stages

Groups are composed of many individuals with different personalities and needs. Generally speaking, though, groups develop an identity of their own. In so doing, they tend to go through a series of stages. While it is possible that all groups will not go through the same stages, the following are the group stages elaborated by Cohen and Smith (1976). Knowing where your group and the individuals in the group are in the process can help in structuring your facilitation.

Stage 1: Acquaintance

Individuals are looking for something in common, a way to categorize one another. Outside roles and statuses often determine inside roles. Group members share names, background, residence, occupations, likes, and dislikes. This is a time of sizing up each other and thinking "Am I going to fit in here?"

Stage 2: Goal Ambiguity and Diffuse Anxiety

Group members may feel confusion, uncertainty, anxiety, and difficulty in understanding directions or the purpose of group activities. Members may feel very unsure of themselves. Some may feel helpless and become self-deprecating and express inadequacy. Some members will attempt to establish bonds with others who seem to have similar problems, interests, attitudes, and backgrounds. Self-centered communication, hesitant and resistant behaviors may also be noted. The situation is new and ambiguous, so values and attitudes may go into a state of flux.

Stage 3: Members' Search for Position

Power may shift rapidly during this stage as various assertive members try to influence and/or control the group or engage in leadership struggles. The initiators become leaders, while fearful members may intellectualize and generalize. Indirect discussions and outside concerns are focused on rather than here and now tasks or feelings. The first here and now feelings expressed tend to be negative, frequently toward the leader or the course. This may be in the form of a challenge. There's fear in this stage of discussing the real self. Anger may be at the perceived dependence on the leader.

Stage 4: Sharpened Affect and Anxiety—Confrontation

In this stage, some individuals may clash with one another for leadership, while others may play more passive roles. Anxiety and fear are expressed by anger and defensiveness. This may feel like a mutiny to you, or it can be as simple as one negative statement by one individual. Interactions may only focus on tasks, with isolation or cliques forming after the endeavors. If you successfully handle the negative feelings, the group then has permission to get more positive and intimate. You need to be able to say, "I hear that you are angry at me"; or "I see that you are overwhelmed by the demands of the course; can you tell me more about it?" This is an important stage for leaders.

Stage 5: Sharpened Interactions—Growth

Original group leaders re-emerge. Some members behave in ways that encourage total group involvement. Group members become more involved. Misunderstandings are sharpened as frequent communication occurs. Group members share significant personal experiences. Here and now concerns about power and leadership develop. Trust grows between you and the group and within group members. Members begin to talk more openly and test their perceptions and assumptions with you and others.

Stage 6: Norm Crystallization

Norms develop as the group works on and evolves rules and standards for behavior in the group. Group attention stays on interaction and processes within the group, not on outside matters. One person may assume the role of disciplinarian who punishes group members deviating from the group norms. Daily routines are established and members become self-disciplined and self-regulated. A unique culture develops that includes jargon, rituals, and group consciousness and cohesion. In general, there is a willingness to work together on tasks and goals. Individual identity is submerged in the group. Members subjugate their own identity in pursuit of group unity.

Stage 7: Distributive Leadership

Members accept each other as equals. Members accept the authority of your role and there is less black and white thinking in regard to you. Group members will use you more freely as a "skilled resource" who can observe the group process and help them deal with personal issues. You will be seen as a person and as a member of the group.

Figure 8. Crossing the Acid River

Members become observers of the group process and thus become more self-regulating and self-determining. Decisions become more based on consensus. When conflict occurs, it is over substantive rather than hidden issues. Formalized structure tends to dissipate and informality prevails.

Stage 8: Decreased Defensiveness and Increased Experimentation

There tends to be a dropping of masks and protective facades at this stage. Insight into others develops and becomes common. There is a freer flow of feelings and thoughts. Tension and expressions of negative and positive feelings are expressed and worked through in a more open manner. Members tell each other their reactions and perceptions. There is an increase in empathy and a nonjudgmental atmosphere prevails. Less regard for power and status exists in the group. Group members discuss and work on personal problems. They try out new ways of behaving. Risk taking increases and members have better self-esteem. Members are more willing to compromise for greater solidarity.

Stage 9: Group Potency

The group in this stage accepts individual members and rewards their positive changes. Members know when it's appropriate to use the group. Cooperation and shared responsibility is common. Interdependence increases interpersonal solidarity. The loyalty and affection to each other is increased. The group may deal with highly intense interpersonal interactions without becoming defensive or changing the subject. Intense joy and pleasure are also experienced. Members become confident the group will accept them as they are. The members also accept the group as a potent change agent.

Stage 10: Termination

There are expressions of over-optimism about the power of the group. Individually and collectively the members are optimistic. Denial of the impending termination is expressed by disbelief and regret. As a defense against the pain of separation, some members withdraw before the group actually ends. Other members experience happiness over leaving and returning to the outside world. Still others attempt to plan ways for the group to get together in the future. Testimonials to the power of the group and the experience are expressed. Some members feel they have completed the task of the group and are ready for the outside world, while others continue to explore the mechanics of the transfer of learning.

As the course ends and the group terminates, it may be useful to talk about the death of the group and how individuals deal with grief in their lives. The group will never be the same, and developing some rituals and giving students the opportunity to share their feelings and learning with each other will help to bring some closure to the group. You can discuss how individuals make contact in their lives and what "letting go" of the connection feels like for them.

Leader Interventions

The primary responsibilities of a leader of adventure-based learning experiences include overseeing safety parameters, providing skills instruction, and facilitating personal development. To adequately meet these responsibilities you may use a variety of interventions. Nine different types of leader interventions that have been adapted from Dyer (1972) can be used to structure and process the experience. They are provided below. Your educational background and training as well as the situations that arise with groups will determine which interventions can be carried out with the most comfort.

1. **Content Focus:** This entails some specific introduction of information into the group focus. The information may include safety issues, providing clear guidelines and parameters, addressing participant concerns and expectations, sharing an experience, giving an opinion, or clarifying some instructions. Content interventions are most helpful when they provide information the group members feel they require to proceed with the activity or exercise. For example: (a) "Today's hike is going to be challenging. I would like you to monitor the statements that you make to yourself when you are feeling stretched" or (b) "On this activity you have a twenty minute time limit. Then, we will take some time to discuss how decisions were made."

Figure 9. Setting Parameters for an Activity

23

2. *Process Focus:* This intervention focuses on what is happening within the group. It looks at the interactions among members while they are doing certain tasks. You want to focus on the here and now process in the group. Examples may be (a) "How are you working together as a group?", (b) "I wonder why some people aren't sharing their feelings or ideas", (c) "It seems like the same people do all the work", (d) "What is preventing people from speaking their mind?", (e) "It seems like the group is more concerned with getting the task done rather than with how it's done", or (f) "Right now I experience a lot of tension in the group."

3. *Eliciting Feelings:* This intervention helps members develop a sense of being a group. It may not only let members know that they are not alone, but also may help them see how others feel about their behavior. Reluctance to share feelings may be based on lack of trust, self-confidence, or inability to identify feelings. An example of this intervention may be, "How did you feel, Mary, when the group rejected your suggestions?"

4. *Sequencing Activities:* Making decisions about course components and the order that they should occur is an important aspect of establishing a positive learning environment. Some of the important questions that you will want to ask yourself include: How does the activity relate to the group and individual goals that have been set? Is the group mentally and physically prepared to do the activity? Do they have the ability to attempt the activity or to complete it? What is the general mood of the group? What types of positive and negative interactions are affecting the group? How cooperative are the group members? What is the physical shape and abilities of the participants? How tired are they? What is the group's developmental stage and level of functioning?

Figure 10. Providing Skills Instruction

5. *Direct Feedback:* In a group, members are usually anxious to know how you view them. These concerns may be a legitimate request for feedback or may indicate that the participants have not worked through viewing you as an authority figure. Feedback is very important in the group process. It's important that members not only get it from you but also from their peers. You can facilitate this by asking, "Ernie, how do you interpret or view Bill's behavior now?" Once a few viewpoints are expressed, then you can respond. If the group is protective of its members, you may want to go first and then ask others for their feedback. Once the group coalesces, the group members will begin to give each other direct feedback without you having to do so.

6. *Cognitive Orientation:* At times, you may want to offer participants a relevant theory or information in order to provide them with a conceptual framework for understanding group process. Suggestions for topics include problem-solving techniques, group stages, how to express feelings, assertive behavior, defining forgiveness, and leadership styles. The extent to which you use the cognitive orientation intervention will depend on your need to be seen as an expert, as well as an assessment of how best to help group members learn.

7. *Performing Group Functions:* You may intervene by using task maintenance functions. The purpose of these interventions is to help the group maintain itself as an effective system that continues to promote learning. One way to do this is to have the group reflect upon and analyze what they have just done. You will facilitate this by asking for opinions or reactions. For example, you might say, "O.K. what is working here?, what is not working?, and what do you need to do to be more efficient?" Generally, you will reduce such interventions as participants develop a greater ability to perform these functions.

8. *Diagnostic Intervention:* When a group is having difficulty getting started or working together, you may diagnose what you see happening in the group. An example of a diagnostic intervention would be: "There may be a number of possible reasons to explain why the group is disintegrating. The goals may be too vague. Another is that individuals may be afraid of revealing themselves because they may be criticized. Are there any other possible reasons that you think may exist?" The diagnostic intervention encourages participants to use a diagnostic approach in order to better understand the group process.

9. *Protective Intervention:* In some groups, members may want to share deep emotional issues (e.g., incest, physical abuse, or rape) that extend beyond the boundaries of the group. These personal emotional issues may significantly diverge from the goals of the group. In addition, you may not have the appropriate training to deal with such issues. Therefore, you will want to intervene and possibly choose to speak with the member individually and encourage him or her to contact a professional counselor or psychologist. You also want to intervene when one or two members are being cruelly criticized. In general, you are responsible for protecting the emotional safety of each of the group members.

Enhancing Communication Skills

Communication can be defined as "a dynamic and ongoing process in which people share ideas, information, and feelings" (Egan, 1986, p. 73). A number of factors influence the communication process as it occurs between leaders and course participants. In this section, we will highlight some verbal and nonverbal behaviors that affect the quality of communication. They include the use of attending behaviors, active listening, noticing nonverbal behavior, using I-messages, empathic responses, and giving feedback. If you understand and can use these communication skills, you can interact positively with people that you come in contact with.

Developing Attending Behavior

Attending skills indicate that the listener is physically and emotionally present and listening. These specific behaviors assist in establishing and maintaining a good rapport, and also put you in a good place to be an active listener. Some specific attending behaviors and a brief explanation of each follow. Please keep in mind that these are generalizations and may vary as a result of cultural differences.

Nonverbal Cues

1. **Eye Contact**—Focus your eyes directly on speakers but be sensitive to the effect such direct eye-to-eye contact may have. Many people feel uncomfortable with direct eye contact and tend to shy away from it. Readjust your focus accordingly.

2. **Facial Expressions**—Your expressions or lack of them provide feedback to speakers, thereby prompting them to say more, to slow down, to clarify. More important, let your face tell speakers that you empathize with him or her. Smiles, frowns, expressions of surprise or disappointment don't cost much so share them with others. Simultaneously, attend to the facial expressions of speakers. What nonverbal messages are being conveyed?

3. **Body Posture**—You can help speakers relax by relaxing your own body. Body gestures often convey meaning. When listeners lean toward or touch speakers, a high level of interest and involvement is communicated. Attend to the body language of speakers—it also is sending messages.

4. **Physical Space**—The distance that people create between themselves has an inherent communication value. While this may vary due to cultural differences, it has

27

been described that an 18-inch distance between speakers is "intimate space", the 18-inch to 4-foot distance is "personal space" and the 4-foot to 12-foot distance is "social distance." Each of these distances communicates distinct nonverbal messages.

Verbal Cues

1. **Silence**—When used appropriately silence is a valuable asset to communication. It can give both parties a chance to stop and reflect on what has been said. It may encourage speakers to say more. Too often listeners feel compelled to make an immediate response and, consequently, they begin searching for a reply before speakers have concluded. Wait a few seconds to be sure that speakers have completed their thoughts.

2. **Brief Verbal Acknowledgement**—It is valuable to occasionally interject brief verbal acknowledgements, such as: "I see," "Uh-huh," "Oh," "That's too bad," etc. The goal is to express interest and concern without interrupting or interjecting personal comments. Keep the reaction brief and quickly refocus on the speaker.

3. **Paraphrasing**—When appropriate, summarize the essence of what speakers have said in a sentence or two. By feeding back to speakers the gist of their message, you validate the communication. It gives the people that you are communicating with direct feedback as to how well you understand the message. In addition, it communicates to senders that you want to understand what they are saying. It indicates that you care about them enough to listen carefully and that you are interested in what they are saying. As a result, it often inspires further communication.

Active Listening

In addition to attending to the person that you are communicating with, you will want to really listen to what he or she is saying. Egan (1986) contends that listening has three parts: (1) listening to and understanding verbal messages; (2) listening to and understanding nonverbal behavior; and (3) listening to and understanding the person. As you can see, this involves more than just listening to the words that they are using. It also includes understanding the content, observing gestures, changes in voice and expression, and trying to acquire a sense of the underlying message that is being communicated.

Corey and Corey (1987) suggest that there are some common roadblocks to active listening. They include, (a) not really listening to the person, (b) thinking about what you want to say next instead of paying attention to the person, (c) being overly concerned about how you are viewed by others, and (d) evaluating the individual without putting yourself in the other person's place.

In order to develop active listening skills, you want to focus on the following behaviors:

1. Blocking out external stimuli.

2. Attending carefully to both the verbal and nonverbal messages of speakers.

3. Differentiating between the intellectual and emotional content of the message.

4. Making inferences regarding the feelings experienced by speakers.

Steps in developing the skills of active listening:

STEP 1. Personal Inventory—Effective listening requires that you be aware of your own feelings, prejudices, and expectations about the speaker. In an effort to assess your motivation for being involved with someone, ask yourself: (a) How do I feel about the speaker and the topic to be discussed?, (b) Do I really want to hear what the person is saying?, (c) Do I genuinely want to help the speaker if he or she presents a problem?, and (d) Can I accept the feelings and attitudes of the speaker even if they are different from mine?

Due to the spontaneous nature of most conversations, it is difficult to ask yourself these questions. Try to discipline yourself to ask one or two of these. If the answers are positive, then it becomes easier for you to block out your personal feelings about the speaker and to concentrate on the message being conveyed.

STEP 2. Attending Skills—Establish eye contact, relax and listen. Attend directly to both the verbal and the nonverbal cues of the speaker.

STEP 3. Identifying the speaker's feelings—As the conversation proceeds, try to make private inferences about what the speaker is feeling. Are the verbal and nonverbal messages consistent with each other?

Noticing Nonverbal Behavior

Researchers have stated that nonverbal behavior makes up 75% to 95% of communication (Egan 1986). What people are really saying or meaning can be seen in their posture, facial expressions, tone of voice, excitement level, and mannerisms. When a person is dealing with or talking about something psychologically significant, tactile sensations and body movements are important signals to unconscious feelings or motivations. These signals are not within their awareness and can give you some insight into the student and where to go with him or her for processing and the transfer of learning. Below are some examples of nonverbal information and learning suggested by Norton (1978). Again, it is important to note that these behaviors may vary according to cultural differences.

Head

Stroking hair is a tactile sensation.

Hair hiding face reflects low self-concept or insecurity at that point in the person's life.

Hand on head means the person is holding something back, so ask whether there is more they want to say about the subject.

Eyes

Dry tears (wiping invisible tears) signifies sadness and/or insecurity.

A dominant person maintains eye contact more than the submissive person.

Looking to the side is avoidance.

Looking up is intellectualization or creativity or remembering pictures.

Looking down means the person is dealing with feelings.

Looking up and to the side is looking for approval.

Large irises means the individual is emotionally expressive and sensitive.

Small irises mean that the individual conceals his emotions or thinks with his head rather than his heart.

Mouth

Fingers held to the mouth, stroking the lips, shows a need for nurturance or for support.

Hand in front of the mouth while talking reflects the attitude "I'm not important."

Continual smiling means the person is anxious or nervous and not showing real feelings.

Chin

Person with a strong, extended chin will most often be a stubborn person.

Person with the chin in or recessive tends to be more passive and submissive.

Jaws

A person with a strong chin will also tend to have rigid jaws which show assertion.

Chewing can be an act of hostility, anger, and/or aggression.

Throat

Pulling down is choking off.

Hand on throat is choking off.

Lump represents a need to cry or shout. It may also mean that something is stuck there. There is an unwillingness to "swallow" some feeling or expression imposed on one by other, or an unexpressed wish to tell someone off.

Arms

Crossed arms are holding feelings in.

Holding oneself is a need to be comforted.

No gesturing (arms rigid) shows inhibition of feelings or depression.

Excessive use of arm and hand movements indicates a need for attention.

Hands

Hands represent emotions.

Sitting on hands turned up means the person is tucking in his/her feelings.

Sitting on hands turned down means feelings are being hidden (more severe).

Hands on chest are holding in feelings.

Running fingers or tapping or drumming fingers shows impatience.

Fist and hand show that the person is putting the lid on his/her aggression.

Picking lint is an attempt to be rid of something.

Legs

One leg bounce sometimes means the person would like to kick someone.

Two leg bounce shows impatience or ambivalence.

Rubbing thighs may also precede any conscious feeling or thought about sexuality.

Voice

Soft voice shows lack of self-confidence.

Fluctuating volume—what is said softly is an area where person doesn't feel secure.

Whiny voice shows a need for nurturance, a need to know that people care.

A person with a monotone voice is most likely the type of person who has difficulty making commitments.

Laughing is many times covering up a need to cry.

Talking fast is running from something.

Body Orientation

Body positioned toward the other person, facing the person with forward trunk lean shows involvement.

Lack of involvement is shown by moving away, turning away, backward lean of trunk or by putting any object between the two people.

Using I-Messages

"Dave, I find it hard to believe that you don't know how to read a map by now. Here it is day 7 of the course and you still can't figure out how to orient it."

This is an example of a you-message. When we send you-messages to people, they feel embarrassed, angry, hurt, put-down, or worthless. And, most likely they don't feel like cooperating. You-messages often don't work because: (a) individuals who continually receive negative messages may begin to believe them, (b) when we put the blame for our feelings on others, we risk their refusal to accept the blame and, (c) when we criticize others we may be reinforcing the behavior that they are demonstrating.

When we express our feelings and concerns in I-messages, we appeal to the individual's good nature and desire to cooperate. We are asking for their help. We say, "I'm worried," "I'm concerned," I'm afraid," "I'm disappointed"—and we tell why. We take responsibility for our own feelings and leave the person's behavior up to them. At the same time, I-messages avoid the negative impact that accompanies you-messages, freeing the person to be considerate and helpful, not resentful, angry, and devious.

I-messages meet three important criteria for effective confrontation: (1) they have a high probability of promoting a willingness to change; (2) they contain minimal negative evaluation of the person; (3) they do not injure the relationship.

Constructing I-Messages

I-messages have a definite structure. They focus on the individual's feelings and the other person's behavior, not on the person themself. You are upset with a particular act, not with the total individual. So I-messages begin with "when": they separate the deed from the doer. "When I find the campsite full of trash. . . ." "When people interrupt each other. . . ."

The action that you describe is usually not the real reason for your concern. It is the consequence the behavior produces. So I-messages use "because" to connect your feelings with the upsetting consequences of a person's behavior.

I-messages are composed of three parts:

1. First describe the behavior—Don't blame, just describe. "When we break camp at noon. . . ."

2. Then state your feelings about the possible consequences of the behavior. ". . . I get concerned. . . ."

3. Then state what those consequences are or might be. ". . . that we will be hiking late into the night."

Varying the Format

I-messages can take varied forms. The three parts don't have to be delivered in order, and you may sometimes eliminate the statement of feelings. For example: "When we don't paddle together it becomes difficult to communicate with each other."

Sometimes when you are speaking to an individual student your statement will contain the word "you". It is still an I-message if the "you" is descriptive and not critical or blaming. An example is: "Smitty when you take off down the trail ahead of everyone else, I get worried that you might take a different route than the group and that we'll have to spend lots of time trying to find each other."

Empathic Responses

Empathy is the ability to understand the world of others by "walking a mile in their shoes." Empathy is not the same as sympathy, which entails feeling sorry for someone; rather it is placing oneself in the situation in order to examine how that person feels. Developing an understanding and empathy for what students experience and express is vital if you want to establish a relationship that is based on trust and understanding. This means that you actively listen to hear what feelings are being expressed.

When responding with empathy we attempt to show that we understand as best we can what someone said and how they feel. A common format for formulating empathic responses is to say to the person "You feel _____ or You feel _____ because _____." When first beginning to use empathic responses, you may want to be careful not to sound like you are telling the person how they are feeling, but, rather that you are trying to check with them about what they are saying and feeling. As a result, initially you may want to begin by asking empathic questions such as "Do you feel _____?" or say "It sounds to me like you're feeling _____ because _____. Is that accurate?"

As you become more comfortable with empathic listening and responding you can begin to use the sequence for developing empathy proposed by Carkhoff, Pierce, and Cannon (1980). They suggest that there are four levels of responding to students. Each level encompasses more information as to what you perceive is transpiring for the student. When students feel understood, they will begin to open up more and take more risks into new territory. The four levels of responding are:

Level 1: Responding to Feelings

"You feel sad"

"You feel discouraged"

Level 2: Responding to Feelings and Content—Content puts the feelings in context.

"You feel _____ because _____."

"You feel disappointed because it didn't work out."

Level 3: Personalizing Meaning—What are the implications for the individual?

"You feel _____ because you _____."

"You feel furious because you were criticized; this is (or may be) similar to what happens at home."

Level 4: Personalizing Problems, Feelings, and Goals—What are the implications about the meaning and the problem of the person's feelings?

"You feel _____ because you cannot _____"

"You feel disappointed in yourself because you cannot act immediately on an opportunity and you'd like to"

Early in the course, you can make use of empathic questions, levels 1 and 2 with students, responding to feelings and then adding the content. Level 3 goes deeper or attempts to "anchor" the issues or identify some of the core issues. Level 4 personalizes the problems and the overall goals of the person.

If you can continuously respond at level 2 or 3 to students, they will be assisted in becoming aware of their feelings and will notice the support. This can help them make the breakthroughs that they desire.

It is best to first practice with friends or co-leaders. After beginning to feel comfortable with this form of responding, you can listen for the feelings of students and respond to them appropriately. Ideally, 60–75% of your responses early in the course would be questions, level 1 or 2. This allows students to feel understood as well as to

33

clarify what they are experiencing. At first this method may feel awkward. It is important to try to integrate this procedure into your manner of interacting with course participants. Making these subtle changes can help you become more effective at developing empathy and trust with the students that you work with.

Feedback

Feedback is a way of helping people to consider changing their behavior. It is a way of communicating to people which gives them information about how they affect others. As in the case of a guided missile system, feedback helps individuals keep their behavior "on target" and thus better achieve their goals. The following are some criteria for providing useful feedback:

1. It is descriptive rather than evaluative. Describing one's own reaction leaves individuals free to use or not to use feedback as they see fit. Avoiding evaluative language reduces the need for individuals to react defensively.

2. It is specific rather than general. To be told that one is "dominating" will probably not be as useful as to be told that "Just now when we were deciding which way to go, you didn't listen to what other people said. I felt forced to accept your opinion or be verbally attacked by you."

3. It takes into account the needs of both the receiver and giver of feedback. Feedback can be destructive when it serves only the giver's needs and fails to consider the needs of the person on the receiving end.

4. It is directed toward behavior which the receiver can do something about. Frustration is only increased when people are reminded of some shortcoming over which they have no control.

5. It is solicited, rather than imposed. Feedback is most useful when receivers themselves have formulated the kind of question which those observing can answer. As a group leader, you can ask, "Would you like to hear some feedback?"

6. It is well-timed. In general, feedback is most useful at the earliest opportunity after the given behavior, depending, of course, on such variables as the person's readiness to hear it and support available from others.

7. It is checked to insure clear communication. One way of doing this is to have receivers try to rephrase the feedback they have received to see if it corresponds to what the sender tried to express.

8. When feedback is given in a group, both the giver and the receiver should have an opportunity to check with others in the group for the accuracy of the feedback. Is this one person's impression or an impression shared by others?

In summary, feedback is a way of giving help; it is a corrective mechanism for individuals who want to learn how well their behavior matches their intentions; and it is a means for establishing one's identity—for answering "Who am I?"

Building Rapport

One important way to build rapport is to develop the empathy skills mentioned in the previous section. This section covers another way, that of matching and mirroring. Robbins (1986) states, "People tend to like people who tend to be like them" (p. 9). Matching and mirroring allows students on an unconscious level to think "this person is just like me."

When we communicate, it is contended that only 7% of what is communicated is via the words that we use, 38% is transmitted through tone of voice, and 55% is a result of physiology and body language (Robbins, 1986). Therefore, one way of matching and mirroring is to sit or stand like the person, use the same tonality, phrasing, pitch and mimic their hand gestures, body movements, postures, facial expressions, breathing patterns, and tilt of the head. While it may seem strange to copy the person that we are having a conversation with, it is interesting to note that we all do this unconsciously. We suggest making this practice more intentional.

Another means of matching and mirroring is to use the same words, expressions, or predicate phrases that your students or colleagues use. Here again, they can more easily feel that you hear and understand. Following are some of the words or predicate phrases that students may use. They are divided into visual, auditory, and kinesthetic. Each of us use all three of these ways to communicate, but we usually have a preferred mode.

In general, people with a visual preference talk very fast, their breathing may be high in their chest, and the vocal tone is high-pitched, nasal, or strained. They talk fast because they are making pictures and want to project it out quickly. They use words like: "see," "view," and "paint me a picture." People with an auditory preference speak in more modulated tones; their voices have a clear and resonant tonality. The breathing appears to come from the diaphragm. They use words like: "sounds like," "I hear you," "that rings loud and true," and "to tell you the truth." People with a kinesthetic preference tend to speak in a slow tempo with long pauses between words. Their tonality is low and deep. These people feel as they speak. They use words like: "I want to get a grasp of this," "It doesn't feel right," and "I can't get a hold of what you are saying."

In building rapport and developing trust, if you can identify your students' preferred way of perceiving communication and then match that, students are likely to feel as if you are speaking their language. Add to this the ability to mirror their physiology, body language, and tonality, and rapport can be greatly enhanced. It can be easier then for students to feel the trust in the relationship and to be encouraged out of the circle of comfort to the successes of the new territory.

Predicate Phrases

Predicates are the process words (verbs, adverbs, adjectives) people use in their communication to represent their experiences internally through the visual, auditory, or kinesthetic modality. Listed below are some of the commonly used predicate phrases suggested by Robbins (1986):

Visual (see)	Auditory (hear)	Kinesthetic (feel)
Appears to me	Clear as a bell	Come to grips with
Beyond a shadow of a doubt	Clearly expressed	Control yourself
Bird's-eye view	Earful	Cool/calm/collected
Clear cut	Express yourself	Get a handle on it
Eye to eye	Heard voices	Get in touch with
Horse of a different color	Hidden message	Get the drift of
In view of	Hold your tongue	Hand in hand
Looks like	Idle talk	Hang in there
Make a scene	Loud and clear	Hold it!
Mental image	Manner of speaking	Keep your shirt on!
Mental picture	Purrs like a kitten	Lay cards on table
Mind's eye	Rings a bell	Light-headed
Paint a picture	State your purpose	Not following you
Plainly see	To tell the truth	Pain in the neck
Pretty as a picture	Tongue-tied	Pull some strings
See to it	Tuned in/tuned out	Sharp as a tack
Sight for sore eyes	Unheard-of	Too much of a hassle
Staring off into space	Voiced an opinion	Topsy-turvey
Tunnel Vision	Word for word	Underhanded

Examples that contrast how people with different preferences perceive communication (Robbins, 1986) are found on the following page.

How People Perceive Communication

Generic	Visual	Auditory	Kinesthetic
I understand you.	I see your point.	I hear what you are saying.	I feel that I am in touch with what you're saying.
I want to explain something to you.	I want you to take a look at this.	I want to make this loud and clear.	I want you to get a grasp on this.
Do you understand what I am trying to say?	Am I painting a clear picture?	Does what I am saying sound right to you?	Do you have a handle on this?
I know that to be true.	I know beyond a shadow of a doubt that that is true.	That information is accurate word for word.	That information is as solid as a rock.
I am not sure about that.	That is pretty hazy to me.	That doesn't really ring a bell.	I'm not sure I follow you.
I don't like what you are doing.	I take a dim view of that.	That does not resonate with me at all.	What you're doing doesn't feel right to me.
Life is good.	My mental image of life is sparkling and crystal clear.	Life is in perfect harmony.	Life feels warm and wonderful.

Levels of Processing

When working with individuals, it is frequently difficult to know how to begin and how to help them become conscious of their behavior, thoughts, and feelings. A flow chart that you can use to help focus your attention on the levels of processing is found below. Each level is dependent on processing in order to reach more advanced levels. The level can be viewed as tasks or objectives to obtain, and processing as the vehicle to attain the goal.

The first level focuses on developing an awareness of the unconscious feelings, thoughts, and behavior patterns that get projected onto the experience. You want to help individuals identify and become aware of typical feelings, thoughts, and behavior patterns. Second is the responsibility level. Here participants consciously own their patterns, thoughts, feelings, and actions. In this stage, they become aware of the old patterns. Fritz Perls (1969) called responsibility ''ability to respond.'' This ability to respond leads to a choice at the third level. Individuals can continue with the old patterns or experiment with new emotional, cognitive, and behavioral risks. Experimentation is the fourth level, followed by the fifth level of choice again. Participants choose between maintaining existent patterns or transferring the new learning back to their daily lives at home. Again, processing the experience can help individuals move through each level. Specific exercises and activities that may help you work with individuals progressing through different levels are presented on pages 119 through 129.

Levels of Processing Questions

The following are some examples of questions that will help you facilitate participants' movement through the different levels. The overall intent of these questions is to: a) provide opportunities for new perceptions, new directions, and new options for students; b) have students become interested in their own interaction patterns; c) connect and link the adventure-based experience with transferable knowledge for home application; and, d) have students experiment with new behaviors. Some of the questions use Tomm's (1988) ''circular assumptions,'' Bateson's (1979) ''double descriptions,'' and White and Epston's (1990) approach. Circular assumptions look at the interactional principles and systemic approaches, while double descriptions attempt to get more than one view of the same event and thus open up space for more differences and options. This is not a finite set of questions. Rather, they should be viewed as examples that will help you develop an understanding of the concept and start your own creative processes flowing.

LEVELS OF PROCESSING

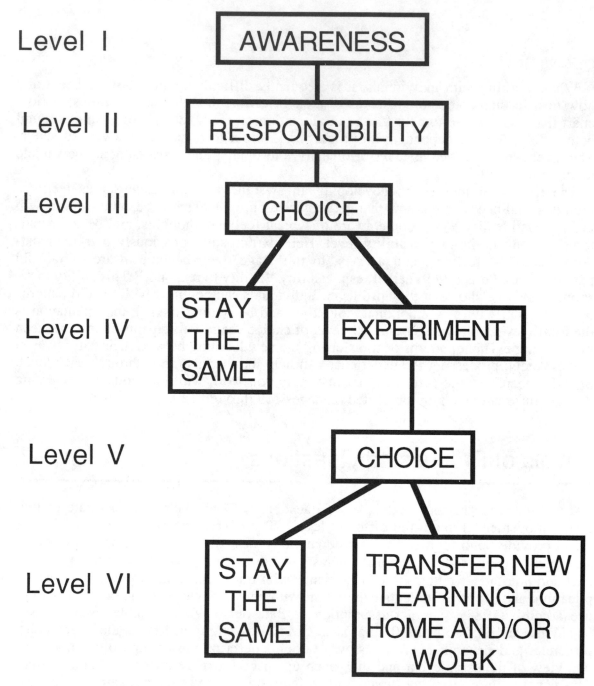

Level I — AWARENESS

Level II — RESPONSIBILITY

Level III — CHOICE

Level IV — STAY THE SAME / EXPERIMENT

Level V — CHOICE

Level VI — STAY THE SAME / TRANSFER NEW LEARNING TO HOME AND/OR WORK

Figure 11. Levels of Processing

Awareness

The objective is to focus on here and now behavior, patterns, and others' perceptions and roles in a non-threatening manner and simultaneously build trust.

Did you notice your role in this activity?

Are you aware that you were (leader, in the background, interrupting others, etc.)

What were you feeling during the experience? What were you stopping from feeling during the activity? How do you feel now?

How did others see (name)'s role in this activity?

When you felt _____, how did you behave?

What was your intention in this activity? Did anyone else notice that?

Did you respond automatically to anything in this activity?

Are you aware of your (point out posture, voice quality, expression, etc.)?

How do others feel when you see (name)'s behavior?

Are you aware that you did _____ again?

Right now I am experiencing you as _____ (angry, defensive, passive, etc.).

Does anyone else experience ____(name)____ as _____?

How can we help you raise your awareness about this pattern?

Who do you think most noticed your role in this activity?

How do you imagine other's react to you when you do _____?

Who in the group do you think was most rooting for your success?

When you did _____, what do you think (name) was experiencing?

What was different about your role or experience?

If you were miraculously able to _____, how would your life be different?

What effect does _____ have in your life?

Responsibility

The object is to have students make the bridge of how their roles and behaviors are similar to what they do at home, school or work. We seek to have them become responsible for what they were previously doing automatically or unconsciously.

Did you notice that you were controlling, withdrawing, interrupting, etc., again? Do you do this at home, school or work?

Is this a typical role for you?

Have others at work or home ever given you feedback about your _____?

I wonder if at home or work when you feel _____, do you _____?

41

What do you think you get out of doing _____ or how does that serve you?

What strengths do you bring to this group?

Do you ever use your strengths to excess?

Can you accept that _____ (controlling, withdrawing, etc.) may be a pattern of yours?

What would it be like if you were always _____ and never changed? How would others respond to you?

Does your style fit in well with others? How do others feel when _____(name)_____ acts this way?

How is your behavior self-protective or self-nurturing?

When you typically do _____ at home, who notices first?

How does your (wife, husband, parents, friends) react when you do _____ at home?

I wonder who else in the group realized that _____ may be a pattern for (name)?

Can you recall a time when you didn't react in this manner? What was different about that situation?

What aspects of this pattern have you felt most pushed around by, and how is this pattern influencing your life?

How long do you want to be pushed around by _____ before you stand up and protest against it?

Who will be the first to notice when you stand up against it?

How much influence does this _____ pattern have over your life? (1–100%)

How much influence do you have over the _____ pattern? (1–100%).

Experimentation

The objective is to give students the opportunity to create new options and choices for themselves.

Are you willing to try something different today?

What would be a risk for you today?

What's preventing you from being more _____ (assertive, expressive, etc.)?

How will you sabotage your attempt to take a new risk today?

Can you tell others in the group what you are going to do today?

How can we support you in your risk today?

How would you evaluate your risk today?

Would you like feedback from others when they see you _____?

With your experimentation what went well? What would you adjust for next time?

How did it feel doing _____(new behavior)_____?

What did you learn by taking the risk?

What was the hardest part about doing _____?

(To others) How do you imagine (name) felt today in trying something different?

What do you think this might tell you about your ability that you wouldn't have otherwise known?

What else do you think you could now do after you successfully completed this risk?

What do you think others will say is the hardest part for you to continue with?

What do you think your risk tells the group that they can appreciate?

Holding the two pictures of yourself, the old you with the _____ pattern and the new you, and comparing them what do you discover about yourself?

Now that you didn't let ___(old pattern)__ push you around, what difference will this make in your future?

Who do you think first noticed you were successful in your experiment?

Who do you imagine is most surprised by your successful experiment?

How much influence do you now feel you have over the _____ pattern (1–100%)?

Generalization and Transfer

The objective is to maximize what has recently been learned so that it can be used back at home, school or work.

What are you blind to, handicapped by, speechless about, etc., at home, school or work?

How can you use this learning at home?

What will prevent you from using what you have learned at home?

What will you need from others to implement your plan at home? What helped on the course?

What are the positive forces that you have at home? How can you enhance them?

What visualization symbol, anchor, or ritual can you use at home to remind you of what you have recently learned on the course?

What statement or affirmation can you use to remind you of what you learned on the course?

Write down goals that you have for yourself at home.

Are you willing to hear feedback from others as to trouble spots that they anticipate for you back at home?

Are you willing to role play some of those trouble spots?

Develop a tool box and describe what's in it to help you attain your goals at home.

When you act differently at home, who will be the first to notice?

What will they see in you that is different?

What will be the first signs for you at home that will tell you you're on the right track?

What do you think it says about you that at home you don't let the _____ pattern push you around anymore?

How will this adventure experience keep you on track at home?

Now that you've tackled the challenges on the course, what issues will you tackle at home?

What do you think your changes at home will tell your (wife, husband, parents, peers) about you?

How much influence will you have over the _____ pattern at home? (1–100%)

What will you need to do to reinforce your influence over ___(old pattern)___?

What aspects of yourself makes you think that you will make significant changes at home?

Methods of Processing

There are many ways to process the adventure-based experience. Many of us are familiar with the approach that involves having a large group sit around in a circle and talk about what they recently went through. This is one effective·technique. Yet, it should not be the only approach that you use. Think about what a house would look like if the only tool that a carpenter had to build with was a hammer. So while the hammer and the large group discussion are important tools for the jobs that you want them to do, they aren't the only ones to use. The following is a short explanation of some different ways that you can use to structure your processing sessions.

Large Group Discussion

This is the approach that most people think of when the word processing comes to mind. There are several different ways for you to structure the discussion. They are:

1. **Open Forum**—within this approach you pull the group together and provide an opening statement in anticipation that the group will volunteer their perceptions and insights. An example of an opening statement that you might want to use is "I'm interested in hearing peoples' reactions to today's peak ascent."

2. **Questioning**—this entails the development of a set of questions that you would like participants to respond to after they have completed the activity. The value of this pre-planning is that you establish specific objectives that you would like to achieve for the session. Through the identification of objectives, you can develop questions that focus in on the specific issues that you would like to see addressed at this time. The sequence of questions that you use will vary according to your personal style. However, we suggest that you begin with the concrete and slowly move on to more insightful types of questions. A general sequence that you may want to consider involves the use of three simple questions: "What happened?", "What did you learn?", "How can you use this knowledge in the future?" Supplemental questions that you may want to consider appear in the section on questions for the levels of processing on pages 39 to 44. Additional processing questions are found on pages 112–116.

3. **Rounds**—a round is an activity in which every member of the group is asked to respond to a stimulus that you have presented to the group. According to Jacobs, Harvil & Masson, (1988) there are three types of rounds. There is the (a) designated word or number round, (b) word or phrase round, and (c) the comment round. The following is a brief explanation of each:

a. **Designated Word or Number Round**—this can be done very quickly since each member is asked to respond with either a single designated word or a number on a scale, which is usually from 1 to 10. A few examples that we have used include: "I would like each of you to think of your role during the last event and choose one of the following labels to describe it: "leader," or "follower." "On a scale from 1–10, how would you rate your commitment to the course right now," or "On a scale from 1–10, how comfortable are you being a member of this group right now? A 1 means that you are not comfortable at all and a 10 indicates that you are very comfortable."

b. **Word or Phrase Round**—in this type of round group members are asked to respond with only a word or a short phrase. A few examples that we have used include: "I would like each of you to think of an adjective that describes how you feel right now," or "I'd like to hear from everyone, so I would like you to think of a word or a phrase that describes how you think we handled the last initiative."

c. **Comment Rounds**—in this type of round group members are asked to share more than a few words, either because the question calls for more than a word or phrase or because there is a desire to have individuals express more than just a few words. Examples that you may want to consider using are: "I would like to hear a brief reaction from each of you about how you feel about your experience on the ropes course? Let's do a round and hear from everyone."

Rounds are a very valuable tool. When time is an issue the use of a designated word or number round or a word or phrase round is really useful for getting people to reflect and communicate in an expedient manner. It also gives the instructor some important information about individuals that you can use as your transition from activity to activity or can follow up on at a later time either individually or with the group. Other advantages of using rounds are that they can be used at the beginning of group discussion to get members focused. Rounds give each person time to think about what they are going to say and also a chance to hear what other people think about the topic of discussion. They also encourage individuals to think in greater depth about a specific issue. As will be discussed later in the section on reluctant individuals, rounds allow you to get everyone involved, and finally the use of rounds permits you as the group leader to survey the group for a general reading of how people are thinking and feeling. This can provide you with a quick survey of how things are going and provide stimulus for deciding what issues to focus on with the group at this time or in the near future.

When using rounds, it is a positive practice to vary the starting point so that different members get to speak first and last. At times you will want to begin with the person who you know is comfortable sharing his or her ideas. This will get the conversation flowing with energy and enthusiasm. This train of thought may also be extended to negative and positive energy people who are members of the group. By beginning with a positive energy person and trying to end with a positive energy individual, you can avoid the pitfall of allowing the negative energy member to shift the focus of the group if that is not appropriate at this given time. Finally, you may want to think about where you want to end the round, especially if you have an individual that you know is reluctant to talk or who you know is in need of some additional time and attention. By ending with that person, you can focus on that member's comments without spotlighting him or her.

Figure 12. Large Group Discussion

Journal Writing

Journal writing is a strong tool that can be used for processing the experience. Journal writing promotes exploration of personal emotional knowledge. Without threat of criticism by an external audience, individuals are free to concentrate on and explore their thoughts and feelings. Writing captures and preserves thoughts and feelings, creating a record of individuals' progression through an experience. The act of writing compels the individual to express in symbols knowledge originally represented and stored in memory in a different form.

Writing, because of its active and personal nature, its cognitive demands, and its feedback characteristics, makes possible unequaled forms of extended and involved thought. Journal writing creates situations encouraging reflection and explicitness, often leading to a renewed awareness of a person's knowledge. Journal writing also promotes an awareness and possible clarification of feelings and emotions.

If you choose to use journal writing as a way to process during a course you will have to provide time for students to do this. If you do not set aside time for students to write, then you can not expect them to find the time on their own. Also, if you want students to use journals, then you must begin very early in the course. Otherwise, it becomes difficult to get students involved at a later time and you have missed a golden opportunity for them to experience a different way to reflect and communicate their thoughts and feelings. When structuring journal writing time, you can choose between using free writing or assigning processing questions. The following is a short explanation of each.

1. **Free Writing**—following an activity or at designated times throughout the course you can ask students to take out their journals and write about what they have recently experienced or their thoughts and feelings about their performance on the course to date. Ask them to find a comfortable spot and to write down what comes to mind. If you want them to share this information with other members of the group, it is important to let them know that before they come back. This way they can decide what they would like to share rather than being put on the spot when they return to the group.

2. **Assigning Processing Questions**—an alternative to free writing is to give students some specific questions that you would like them to respond to in their journal. Again, these can either be kept private or they can be shared with the group after everyone has taken the time to respond individually in writing. Two advantages of assigning questions are that they provide a degree of focus on the issues that you may want to raise and that they also get everyone involved. This is especially valuable when you have an individual or two who tends to sit back. Giving them the questions that you want to discuss prior to the discussion potentially allows them the opportunity to feel more comfortable and confident when the group reconvenes. Some examples of questions that you may want to assign include:

What did it feel like to have your physical safety entrusted to the group or a group member?

How are decisions being made by the group?

What could be done to improve the way that the group goes about solving problems?

What are some of the effective ways of communicating that you used in completing the tasks?

What would you like more of or less of from the group?

What could you do to improve the quality of this experience for yourself?

Figure 13. Journal Writing

Dyads

Dyads occur when you pair up group members to share their perceptions with each other. The value in using dyads is that they allow for more personal interaction. Dyads provide more time for each member to talk and also provide the setting for individuals to discuss things that they may not be comfortable in sharing in a large group setting. Dyads are particularly effective at the beginning of the course to help people become better acquainted and more comfortable with each other. You can structure dyads in several different ways. You can allow group members to choose a person they want to talk with, or you can choose the person to work with. That can be done by having them pair up with the person sitting next to them or by assigning them to be in a dyad with another person. That can be done by saying something like, "We are going to take the next ten minutes to talk about our run through the rapids this morning. I would like Mike and Alice to pair up, Ernie and Linda, Bill and Beth, Kent and Barb and Sue and

Figure 14. Using Dyads During Activity Breaks

Lorraine. Take about five minutes each to talk about what were you feeling and thinking this morning."

When using dyads, you will want to make sure that you give clear directions regarding the topic that they are to discuss. Also, let groups know how much time they have for this discussion. Whenever possible let them know when they have reached the halfway point so that one individual does not monopolize the conversation. In addition, it is a good practice to try and circulate while the dyads are in progress to make sure that they are staying on task. At times, you may want to make yourself a member of a dyad so that you can get to know someone better or if you see that someone is having a hard time. This is a good opportunity to isolate with him or her in order to get a sense of what may be troubling the person.

Small Group Discussion

As an alternative to a large group session or to using dyads, you may choose to use small groups of 3 or 4. Many of the considerations for structuring dyads should be kept in mind when using small groups as well.

Written Activity Sheets

Written activity sheets are papers in which group members are asked to answer questions, fill-in sentence completion items, or make lists in relation to an issue or topic. The advantages of using written activity sheets are that it provides an alternative approach to processing, it focuses attention on the task, provides immediate responses when individuals are done, and, finally it gives people an opportunity to think about what they may want to say before sharing it with the group. As stated earlier, if you want people to share their responses with other members of the group, it is important to let them know that when you give out the activity sheet. An example of a written activity sheet that has been adapted from Hagberg & Leider, (1982) is found in table 1.

An example of a sentence-completion exercise is found in table 2.

Isolation

Providing time for course participants to reflect and communicate with themselves is another form of processing. On Outward Bound courses this time alone, solo, is a standard part of every course. However, you don't have to wait until this designated component of the course to provide individuals with some time to themselves. Concomitantly, when you are instructing shorter courses, eliminating personal time may be a mistake. It is possible to structure short blocks of time to give individuals time to think about what has gone on so far and to get themselves back on track if that is what they need to do. Short blocks of time can be found at several points during short courses—at a vista if you are hiking, spread everyone out and tell them that they have 15 minutes to focus on the hike, the functioning of the group, and/or their performance. The same can be done for rafting or canoeing. On even shorter courses you can find a place for people to take a 15-minute respite, have everyone go off on a solitary walk, or

TABLE 1. Sample Written Activity Sheet

People that have truly helped me in my life are: (include how they have helped you)

Write in the space below all the things you want to achieve in relation to the following factors before you die. Be specific.

Personal (health, fitness, hobbies, education, travel, adventures, etc.)

Career/work (career changes, positions, earnings, special projects, new skills, etc.)

Relationships (family activities, marriage enrichment, friendships, mentors, etc.)

Spiritual (spiritual growth, community service, church activities, people you're interested in helping, etc.)

Lifestyle (type of living situation, geographic locale etc.)

designate quiet time when walking from element to element or from the lunch spot back to the ropes course. The shorter the course, the more important it is to make use of each of those precious minutes.

Drawing

Drawing is another alternative technique that can be used to help individuals get in touch with what is happening on a course. People don't have to develop beautiful pieces of art in order to get in touch with themselves, the group, or the environment. In fact, some of the silliest stick drawings that people develop have great meaning for them and others. A fun activity is to give students time to draw and then to share their drawing with other members of the group. The explanation of words and the visual depiction of those words or concepts are usually a very creative and enjoyable way for group members to share their perceptions. Examples of stimuli that can be used for drawing are:

TABLE 2. Sample of Sentence-Completion Exercises

Today I am

My friends are

Love is

In five years I

I get upset when

When I don't like people I

The hardest thing for me to do is

I am happy when

My hero/heroine is

I feel important when

Life is

During my life, the goals I am going to accomplish are

During this course I want to:

By the end of this course, I hope to:

I find these things easy to do:

I find these things difficult to do:

Some qualities that I like about myself are:

Some qualities that I want to improve about myself are:

Other people see me as:

The ways I'll sabotage this learning are:

Some ways that I can prevent myself from discounting this experience are:

Draw a picture that shows how the group is working together and what your role in the group is.

Draw a picture that indicates what you consider your greatest accomplishment so far in the course.

Draw a picture that shows how you want to feel at the end of this course.

Draw a picture that shows what you would like to gain from this course.

Videotaping

In this era of technological advancement, frequently, there are opportunities to use videotaping as a method of providing stimuli for discussion of thoughts, feelings, and behavior. This is especially true with shorter courses. You can record while the group is planning to solve an initiative activity, while they are implementing the plan, and when they complete the activity. You can begin the discussion of how they attacked the problem and what each person's role in the process was. At the end of the discussion, you can play back the videotape and compare their perceptions with the information on the screen. In addition, participants can set goals for how they want to approach an upcoming activity. The videotape can be used to document their success or lack of success. Finally, you can use the videotape to identify patterns of behavior that you have noticed. This may allow them to move from the level of awareness to that of responsibility.

Increasing Effectiveness

How can our students get the most benefit from the processing sessions that we structure? That is the question that we always want to ask ourselves and our colleagues. The following are some sample suggestions. By no means is it an exhaustive list. Hopefully we can use this as a starting point and continue to add to it as we work with different groups and accrue more experiences.

1. **Structure Regular Periods of Time Throughout the Course.** As pointed out in the introduction, it is important to establish right from the beginning of the course the expectation that we will take time to be introspective and reflective and share our thoughts and feelings. We want participants to consider processing as an integral component of every course.

2. **Vary Style and Method Used.** As a member of the human race we tend to get comfortable with certain ways of doing things. As a result we develop our own patterns and habits. This frequently causes us to do activities, such as processing, in a similar manner all too often. Therefore, we need to become aware of our own behaviors and monitor how we choose to structure our sessions. Make a personal goal to try some of the different approaches delineated in the section on the methods of processing. Using different styles and methods provides for a good change of pace and increases your chances of reaching all members of the group.

3. **Alternate the Times of Day.** For courses that are longer than a day or two, you have the luxury of bringing the group together at various times for the purpose of processing. However, we often wait to process until the end of the day. This decision has a few shortcomings. First, if you get into camp late, processing is the activity that gets eliminated. Second, at the end of a good day of adventure-based experience, people are tired. Often when we bring the group together they begin to ''zone out'' and think about other things (which is frequently a nice warm sleeping bag).

   The suggestion that we are making is not to eliminate using the evening but to make use of other times during the day as well. Spend time before you break camp. Plan a break in the morning or the afternoon. Give students a journal, short solo or dyad break after a high impact activity. Have a group discussion before beginning dinner (increases on-task behavior and succinct discussion) or have one of the instructors get the food cooking while the other facilitates the group discussion.

4. **During Discussion Provide Sufficient Wait Time for People to Think.** There is a tendency for instructors to ask a question and then expect individuals to immediately respond. Research indicates that the mean amount of time that educators wait after asking a question is one second. If individuals are not quick enough to come up with a response, the educator repeats the question, rephrases it, asks a different question or calls on someone to respond. When instructors break out of the pattern

of bombing individuals with questions and increase wait time to five seconds after asking a question, people give longer, more thoughtful responses. More people take the time to think and individuals feel more confident in sharing their thoughts. As a result the quantity and the quality of discussion improves.

5. **Ask Open-Ended Questions.** If you decide to use a processing format in which you want to have a discussion and you choose to ask the group, dyads, or individuals a few questions, it is best to try and ask questions that invite discussion rather than one or two word responses. The first step is to recognize that questions have distinct characteristics, serve various functions, and create different levels of thinking. Questions such as, "Did you enjoy the hike today?" "Who felt that they were challenged today?" call for one word responses. Questions such as "How would you compare today's hike to yesterday's?" and "What personal challenges did you encounter today?" set the stage for students to think in greater depth and provide opportunities for sharing more personal information. An additional consideration when forming questions is to try to be explicit enough to ensure an understanding of your question, but at the same time, try to avoid using so many words that people forget what the actual question is.

6. **Ask One Question at a Time.** On occasion, instructors seeking to get to the meat of a topic or issue will blurt out a series of questions rather than raising a single question, discussing it, and then moving on. For example, "How do you think that you worked as a team and what can you do to improve that in the future?" is a bit too much stimuli. Discussing part one of the question and then, if appropriate, moving to part two is a more effective practice.

7. **Own the Questions That You Ask.** Most of us have gone to school for long periods of our life. Through the process of educational enculturation many individuals come to think of answers to questions as being either the right or the wrong answer. Even though the setting is different, as an instructor of an adventure-based course, you are still the teacher in the eyes of most of the individuals that you will work with. Therefore, many times that you ask a question, course participants will believe that there is a right or wrong answer to the question. So whenever possible, it is a good practice to try to de-emphasize the right or wrongness and set a tone of open discussion. One way to do that is for you to own the questions that you ask. For example, you could begin the discussion by saying "We got into camp late last night; I was wondering if anyone had some ideas about how to remedy that in the future?" or "I'm curious, how did you feel about paddling in whitewater today?" By simply letting them know that this is a personal question it lessens the potential that students will tell you what they think you want to hear.

8. **Give Students Specific Feedback.** As expressed in the section on feedback, page 34, whenever possible try to be specific with your praise and/or criticism. To tell students that they did "a great job today," you have given them a positive message but little more. The day was composed of many hours and many interactions. What aspect of the day made it great? Getting out of their sleeping bags? Putting their packs on? Getting in the rafts? Using the latrine? A more specific statement, such as, "It was super to see the way that you supported each other on the trust fall. You talked about what order to go in. You let the people who expressed concern go first and made sure that everyone was ready before having the person fall. It was enjoyable to see you work together like that."

9. **Guard Against Small Talk.** If you are using the large group format and people begin to have their own private conversations, there are a few things that you can

choose to do. First, you will want to make a quick survey of what may be causing these conversations. Is one person dominating the talk? Has the discussion been dragged on too long? Are you doing all the talking? Are people comfortable sharing their thoughts and feelings with the group? Some interventions that you can consider include (a) making a short comment about the difficulty of listening to someone when other conversations are occurring, (b) asking if people want to divide up into dyads to discuss this point first and then come back to the group (c) establishing a "power object" which is held while talking and placed in the middle of the circle for the next individual to pick up and hold while he or she is talking. Therefore, group members are reminded that only one person should be talking, or (d) terminate the discussion since people are beginning to get scattered and unable to be attentive.

10. **If People Are Not in the Mood, Cut the Session Short.** Making every session into an "encounter group" makes many individuals resistant to getting together for a debrief. Don't try to make every session intense and profound. Don't expect people to talk or push them when they are not ready. It's not uncommon after an intense group meeting for the next group session to be more superficial. If you bring the group together and try to structure a session and you realize that they are not into it, ask if they want to cut this session short or think about using an alternative method of processing, such as rounds or giving people a short isolation opportunity.

Edgework: Creating Breakthroughs to New Territory

As mentioned earlier, disequilibrium is a major catalyst for change. This is true not only for individuals, but for systems and organizations alike. Developments in physics and the natural sciences have led some recent organizational theorists to consider that disequilibrium might be a better strategy for survival in the corporate world than coherence and order (Pascale, 1990). The thrust of this thinking is that the "creative tension" generated by internal differences and new points of view can widen an organization's options and ability to change with the times. Smith (1984) writes that survival requires that organizations periodically "step out" of well-worn routines created and reinforced by past success.

In an effort to attenuate the disequilibrium, an individual or organization may experiment with a new mind set, product, or action and experience success. It is in the brief moment or moments prior to a unique action or "breakthrough" that the ingredients for change are found. Here in these moments also resides information that will facilitate the transfer of learning from this success to other successes, for the individual and the organization. This section will explore how to process the experience for these breakthroughs.

One of the cornerstones of experiential education is that we encourage people to try things that they wouldn't generally do on their own. In other words, they leave their safe, familiar, comfortable and predictable world for uncomfortable new territory. Like the pioneers and explorers who traveled to the Old West in search of fortune, we hope the adventures of our students also will lead them to "gold." When they find the gold, we assume that they will locate additional treasures in the new territory. The assumption that the gold is the sole treasure to be gained from the journey is limiting. In actuality, it's the struggle of the journey between the known and unknown where the "gems" for future learning reside.

What is gained from the struggle can lead to learning that can be used in the future. At the "edge" is where many explorers turned back, because of the lack of water or food, battles with the Indians, or an inability to endure and tolerate the continual fears and apprehensions. Breaking through the edge into the realm of possibilities and the land of gold was thereby suppressed. It is at the edge of the breakthrough where processing the experience is most important. Figure 15 represents the journey between the two worlds, where individuals choose to either turn back or break through. Figure 16 attempts to show how personal growth or stretching previous risky and unknown experiences can be tamed and incorporated within the comfortable and safe zone, thus enhancing one's self-esteem.

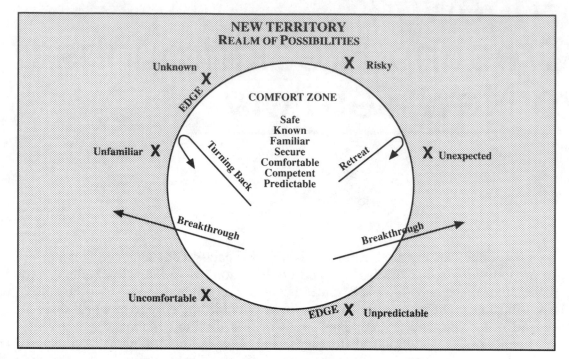

Figure 15. Breaking Through Limits to New Growth

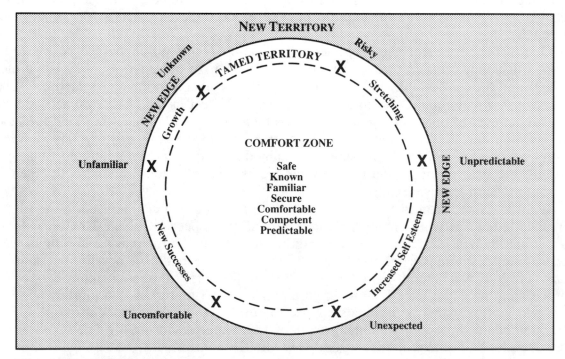

Figure 16. Growth

So what happens at the edge? As people get closer to this unknown, new territory, their sense of disequilibrium increases and a sense of uncertainty exists. As mentioned earlier, the wall of defenses and habitual patterns become prominent in an effort to control the sense of disequilibrium. In addition, peoples' feelings intensify at the edge; they may be fearful, anxious, confused, excited or feeling alone. Their physiological symptoms change, palms sweat, hearts race, respiration quickens, pupils dilate, posture stoops, faces become flush, and individuals may pace.

Also, the internal conversation we all have with ourselves gets louder, and our self-limiting beliefs may surface, such as, "I can't do this"; "I won't"; "I'll fail"; "I'm stupid"; "I'll make a fool of myself"; "I must do it perfectly"; "Life is hard"; "The company has always done it this way"; "What will others think of me?"; or "There must be something wrong with me." At the edge is also where feelings may be communicated via metaphors, such as "I feel like I'm about to be shot"; "I have a weight on my chest"; "I feel paralyzed"; "I feel dead inside"; or "It's like my heart is going to jump out of my body." All of these things happen in a split second at the edge, and the individual either breaks through and takes the leap or turns back to safe territory.

A wealth of valuable information is lost when we wait until everyone has completed an activity before asking individuals to reflect and process. Participants have experienced strong mental, emotional, and physiological changes, yet, by the time we have made time to discuss it with them, they have returned to equilibrium without developing a true awareness of what they recently experienced. As a result, future struggles at the edge are devoid of this knowledge, and they may simply react to these symptoms rather than act on, act with, or act in spite of them. The impact of repeating these same patterns without realizing it in the future may be poor business decisions, lost profits, inability to perform at the same level, relapse, low self-esteem, or attributing successes to luck or chance.

Some pioneers turned their wagons around and headed back East without realizing that they may have been only moments or miles away from gold or success. Similar missed opportunities have most likely happened to us and to our students as well. We can try to offset these missed opportunities by doing "edgework" and processing for breakthroughs. In essence, we heighten the possibility of promoting change by using more of the experience as stimuli for growth and development.

The Moments Before Success

Typically, we process what happened after the activity or success, which we'll call S+1, the moments after the success. This is still very valuable and can be greatly enhanced when we explore what happened right after the edge, or the moment or moments before the success, S-1. Usually these moments pass quickly without the awareness of individuals and are generally lost for current and future learning. What we are advocating is putting this moment or moment at the edge under a microscope and examining the feelings, patterns, conversations, physiology, beliefs, support, and metaphors that encompass these moments. In effect, what we want to do is slow down or freeze the moments before the success or the retreat, so that individuals' thoughts, feelings, and actions that make up their strengths and/or weaknesses become conscious and communicated. We want to know what specifically happened at S-1 to allow for a successful leap, or what did the person do to retreat to safer territory? Herein lie the golden nuggets to be treasured and used again and again when the course is over and new edges in other settings are approached.

In some circumstances, S-1 can be a split second, where, in other activities, S-1 may last from a few minutes up to an hour. Some examples of the S-1 experiences include:

1. Walking across the "beam" on the ropes course, where the emotions are at their height. There may be a brief S+1 respite at the end of the beam before a new S-1 experience on the next event.
2. Being blindfolded in an activity for the first time will engender disequilibrium, tension, or anxiety.
3. The moments while the group is confused, frustrated, or anxious before figuring out how to solve a problem-solving activity.
4. The moments on the perch before jumping for the trapeze bar while on the pamper pole exemplifies being on the edge with all its encompassing intensity.
5. You've talked about rock climbing and provided instruction in the area of climbing techniques and style. The frightened look in your students' eyes as they look at the upcoming climb tells you that they are at S-1.

The experience and processing can be viewed in the following manner:

S-1	S	S+1
A. The edge	Success	A. Moments after the success
B. Freezing the moments before the success	or	B. Reflection about experience
C. Discovery of the success or retreat chemistry	Breakthrough	C. What can be taken away from the experience
D. Examining the components or ingredients		

Figure 17 is a graphic that identifies factors or components to look for when S-1 is put under the microscope.

Processing at S-1

The following are thoughts and strategies that you can use to gather information about what happens the moment before a success or retreat. There are two parts to this process: (a) what did happen either to promote or inhibit a success, the ingredients or components existing at S-1; and (b) what the individual can bring to the edge to increase the likelihood of a success. We'll explore each of the major components of S-1, stated earlier.

First of all, using our levels of processing model, we want students to be aware of what is happening at S-1. How do they sabotage their efforts or encourage their successes? Next, in the responsibility level, we would like them to own these patterns, conversations, feelings, etc., and establish that these are typical responses. At the experimentation level, students try new behaviors or strategies. When at the edge, they can utilize these new sources. And finally, with generalization and transference, students can predict how they'll respond at new edges at home or work and be able to suggest resources or strategies to employ to bring about peak performances. Using some of the levels of processing questions can be valuable at times of S-1.

As part of the awareness level, you can share with students the model presented here. When risks are taken or we go from the known to unknown territory we come to the edge of what is no longer comfortable. Students can be taught to expect and be prepared

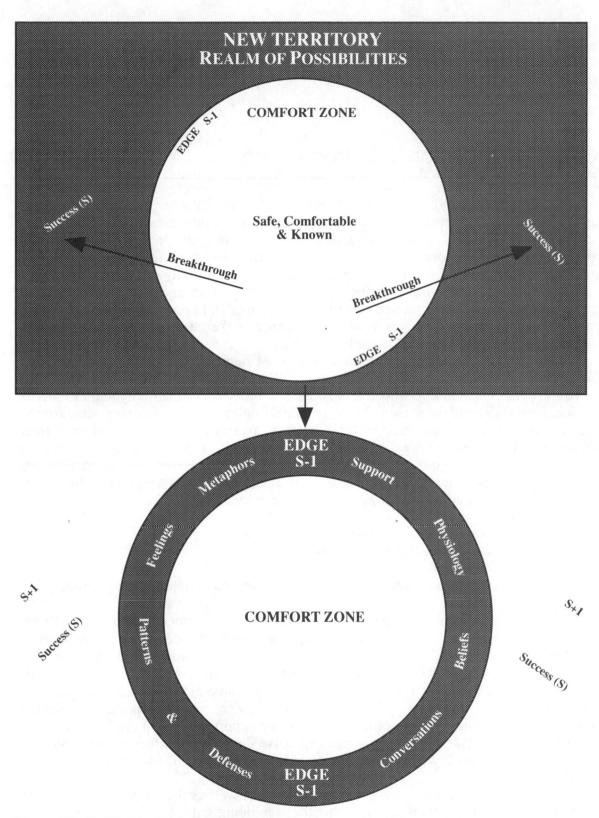

Figure 17. Putting the Edge Under the Microscope

for intensity in their feelings, conversations, physiology, and self-limiting beliefs. You can describe some of the main signs and symbols they will have at the edge in other situations as well. The objective here is to have students identify when they are at the edge and become aware of what specifically they are doing at these moments and decide if it is helpful or hindering.

Cardinal Rule for S-1 Processing

Whenever possible, you want to stop or freeze the activity when you see individuals or the group at heightened emotional levels. This is when they are in S-1; usually they are frustrated, confused, tired, excited, or stuck. By stopping the process, you give them an opportunity to explore what they are experiencing—what is happening at this moment before the answer, solution, or breakthrough occurs. Usually one or two words describing what is transpiring is sufficient. This gives you an anchor or benchmark to come back to later, when you are in S+1. Your group should come to expect this interruption as a means to discover what is happening at the edge, so they can take this learning back to the school, office or home.

When working with mental health or chemical dependency groups, the preferred question to ask when you stop the group is "What are your feelings right now, in a word?" It is at these moments before a success or retreat that relapse dynamics emerge for a chemical-dependent person or dysfunctional coping mechanisms may arise for the mental health client. Awareness of their feelings, actions and thoughts and their interrelationship can provide a wealth of therapeutic material. Corporate groups will require a different set of questions at S-1. We don't want to alienate some of the participants with "touchy-feely" language, yet we need to focus on what is transpiring. Some examples of questions at S-1 for corporate groups may include:

1. "What are you experiencing right now?"
2. "What is happening for you right now?"
3. "What is going on for you now?"
4. "Go inside for a moment and discover what information or data you are generating."

The metaphors for corporate groups at S-1 are that these moments simulate the "chaos" in the company that Tom Peters (1987) writes about, the job stress, or demands of the workday, when deadlines are fast approaching, resources are cut back, and communication is strained. Peters (1987) writes, "The winners of tomorrow will deal practically with chaos, will look at the chaos per se as the source of market advantage, not as a problem to be gotten around. Chaos and uncertainty are market opportunities for the wise" (p. xiv). Being unaware of these stressors or opportunities and one's reactions to them can lead to cost overruns, poor and expensive decisions, ineffectual performances where products must be redesigned, low morale and motivation, and strained interpersonal relationships.

The next line of questions for most populations, as well as the corporate groups and mental health groups, has to do with what they are doing with their feelings or experiences. In order to help students use the information that they currently have, you may want to ask questions similar to these: "Now that you are aware of what is going on for you, is there anything that you want or need to say to the group?" "What risk could you take to help you and the group have a success?" These questions access the responsibility and experimentation levels.

In summary, even though you may stop your group for only two to three minutes while in S-1, this is the space that holds valuable ingredients for their successes or the obstacles for their failures. These few moments can give you a treasure chest full of gems to process that your students can exchange for future achievements at school, home or the office.

Edge Components

Below are the main components at S-1 that you want to help your group become aware of and eventually alter or refine in order to become more encouraging, positive, and supportive so future breakthroughs at the edge are possible. Many of these signs and symptoms overlap and influence each other but are presented individually.

1. Defenses and Typical Patterns

As mentioned earlier, the defenses or patterns that emerge as protection against the anxiety or fear of hurt and rejection are generated from being in disequilibrium. At the edge, it is important to make conscious these unconscious responses, patterns, or actions. These behaviors and responses were at one time successful in combating the anxiety. However, currently they typically are outdated, limiting, and no longer useful.

For most of us, between the ages of seven and ten, we made rules or guidelines for how to control or manage our lives. These rules helped us get out of uncomfortable situations. We may have made a joke, or become angry, isolated or intellectualized. When this worked, we felt relieved and reinforced to use this again in other difficult situations. As a result, we tend to rely on this pattern or defense automatically in uncomfortable situations. The problem arises when this pattern is not as useful anymore and we still cling to it. Retaining these patterns is similar to having a computer that when initially introduced was state of the art technology. Now we continue to use that same computer for 15 to 20 years without updating it. While it still functions, it is no longer as efficient or effective as some recently developed models. Another analogy would be using old eight-track tapes over and over again and refusing to accept that compact discs sound better. The same concept applies to our fixed defenses or patterns. Our experiences, knowledge and capabilities have enhanced and improved since we were younger; therefore, it is time to renovate our user patterns.

Adventure-based courses, which put individuals on the edge, can challenge students to update, refine, and alter mental programs when they emerge. An effective means to bring about these shifts is to use the awareness and responsibility level of processing questions and/or the activities at the end of the book. Students can be encouraged to experiment with new behavior patterns when at the edge.

2. Feelings

Feeling are important for us to be aware of, understand, and befriend. Many of us have learned to "not feel" and haven't learned to feel, manage, and sometimes just tolerate feelings when they are uncomfortable, unfamiliar, and negative. (See "Feelings Aren't Biodegradable" section for more information on feelings.) What we have learned is to stuff, run from, and avoid feelings. Feelings are going to intensify when we get closer to new territory at the edge. We get anxious, uncomfortable, impatient, scared, excited, confused, and vulnerable while in S-1, to name just some of the feelings.

Each person has their unique set and sequence of feelings which will typically emerge when arriving at new territory. The awareness and responsibility for these feelings will help demystify these emotions and move them from being an enemy to being an ally. Because these feelings are intense while on a course, we have a great opportunity to help students feel and learn from their emotions. What are the specific feelings each student experiences when at the edge? By the end of the course, each student should know what their feelings are, how they typically respond to their feelings, and what happens when they experiment with new reactions to these core feelings.

Brian Tracy (1987) stated that we are born with just two fears—fear of falling and fear of loud noises; the remainder we have learned. On a course we can help students unlearn some of their fears. Some of these fears are of deeper emotions, like fear of rejection, embarrassment, grief, loneliness, horror, inadequacy, and sadness. It is the fears that emerge and intensify at the edge that we must help our students break through.

Susan Jeffers (1987), in her book, *Feel the Fear and Do It Anyway,* gives the prescription for breaking through the edge in her title. She also states, "At the bottom of every one of your fears is simply the fear that you can't handle whatever life may bring you" (p. 15). She suggests five statements about fear that may be helpful to share with students who are doing edgework:

1. "The fear will never go away as long as I continue to grow.
2. The only way to get rid of the fear of doing something is to go out . . . and do it.
3. The only way to feel better about myself is to go out . . . and do it.
4. Not only am I going to experience fear whenever I'm on unfamiliar territory, but so is everyone else.
5. Pushing through fear is less frightening than living with the underlying fear that comes from a feeling of helplessness." (Jeffers, 1987, p. 30).

Once students have identified and expressed their feelings, the next step is to go ahead and do it anyway, even though they may be scared, confused, or helpless. For example, if students can learn to feel the feelings and move forward with them, they will experience more breakthroughs and successes. Feelings, will become information for them, rather than impediments to their progress or reasons to retreat. This information is like knowing how your car is running while on a trip. It's important to know how much fuel you have, if the emergency brake is on, what the tire pressure is, or if the car is running hot, so you can make any adjustments and keep moving rather than stopping or turning back. Feelings, then, are a gauge to be read and be aware of rather than a flashing red light that means DANGER and STOP.

3. Physiology

People's physiology can give information on how and what they are feeling at the moment. Their physiology is analogous to the red light in a car that signifies something is going on under the hood and may need exploring. For our purposes, physiology will mean the internal cues of the physiological symptoms, like one's heart racing, face flushing, sweating, respiration quickening, and pupils dilating, along with external signs like one's posture, gait, voice tonality and quality, mannerisms, and eye contact. At the edge, an individual's typical physiology patterns will intensify.

When processing at S-1 you want to raise your students' awareness of what information their physiological symptoms give them. These signs are usually unconscious re-

66

sponses to a situation, and we want our students to become conscious of them. There will be a specific sequence and typical pattern to these signs whether the situation is speaking in front of a group, preparing for a rock climb, or reporting to their boss. These kinds of situations may arouse the feeling of anxiety.

For example, when Betsy felt anxious, her heart would pound, her palms would sweat, she would look down, have shallow breath, and speak in a soft, tenuous voice. Being aware of and understanding this pattern allowed Betsy to have more choices in managing this feeling rather than the feeling managing her. Betsy experimented with new patterns when at the edge in later activities. When anxious, she stood tall, took deep and confident breaths, focused her eyes on what she was afraid of, and told herself in a powerful voice, "I can do this." We had her practice saying this out loud, along with changing her physiology many times. She was able to relax more, use this anxious energy constructively, and move forward through the edge where she had previously chosen to turn back. For Betsy, these physiological signs became signals that she was anxious and triggered the association of what she needed to do to manage this emotion and stay on track. This example illustrates how we can help students bring new resources to the edge to accomplish their goals both on the course and in other settings.

There is a reflexive quality between feelings and physiology, each influencing the other. We first want to help students become aware of what signs go with what feelings. These signs then become the cloud formations which indicate what kind of weather or feelings are present. Second, we encourage students to change their postures, breathing patterns, and mannerisms to elicit new feelings and empower them to move through previous road blocks. Stopping the process in S-1 helps identify these signs or symptoms which may have gone unnoticed and are therefore unavailable as a possible new resource for the person.

4. Beliefs

Beliefs are the mental or cognitive maps that we use as our guidelines to stay on the safe and secure trail within our comfort zone. They are made up of a network of premises and presuppositions. Our defenses, patterns, or actions, described above, are the means we use to stay oriented. These beliefs, like our defenses, were formed early in our life and may have been influenced or reinforced by our family and friends. Today, they may be self-limiting beliefs, when earlier in life they may have been necessary for survival and very useful.

In this text, we have called these patterns of thoughts: beliefs, cognitive maps, and mind-sets. Thomas Kuhn (1962), in *The Structure of Scientific Revolution,* called these mental models a "paradigm." He defines a paradigm as "A constellation of concepts, values, perceptions and practices shared by a community which forms a particular vision of reality that is the basis of the way a community organizes itself" (p. 11).

What is important to recognize in this definition is the shared nature of a belief system. On an adventure-based course, the group can become the community which organizes itself around a new paradigm or shared vision of reality. So, aside from the new perspectives individuals obtain from being at the edge and breaking through to new territory, the community is a supportive audience or hungry critics. As a facilitator and change agent, you have the difficult task of helping individuals move into new territory, acknowledging personal achievements, along with shaping the community or group to be receptive, encouraging, and supportive, which may be a paradigm shift for the group at large.

Paradigms are very powerful in their makeup. There are many basic assumptions in life that drive us, without our conscious awareness. In essence, we may be seeing everything in our lives through smudged glasses, which we don't realize are even on our face. Kuhn (1962) observed three paradigm patterns. First, the dominant paradigm is seldom, if ever, stated explicitly; it exists unquestioned. Second, once the paradigm is accepted, it is clung to tenaciously by our mental apparatus. Third, the unfolding of a new paradigm is always discontinuous, meaning that it is characterized by interruptions or breaks and thus difficult to own or believe.

Intellectual and emotional resistance inevitably arise when a radical way of perceiving the world is presented (Barker, 1985). What this means to you as a group leader is that facilitating for awareness and responsibility of beliefs will be very challenging because, first, students don't realize they are operating from these beliefs; second, there is a lot of comfort from these paradigms and, conversely, resistance to looking at their world without their smudged glasses.

Below is a list of some of the common beliefs that can be self-limiting for individuals. They are drawn from the work of Nemeth (1990), Ellis (1975), and Burns (1980). Your challenge is to facilitate students' awareness, responsibility, and experimentation of and with the beliefs that emerge at the edge. There will usually be one core belief that fits best and other beliefs that are layered around this assumption. This core belief typically will not feel good to the individual, and that is why they will consciously or unconsciously compensate for it. Examples of core beliefs are:

1. "Something is wrong with me."
2. "I can't."
3. "I won't."
4. "I'm stupid."
5. "People are jerks."
6. "Life is hard."
7. "I don't know."
8. "I'll do it my way."
9. "I must be unfailing, competent and perfect in all I do."
10. "It's absolutely necessary that I'm loved and approved of by everyone."
11. "It's horrible when things are not the way I want them to be."
12. "External events cause all my misery."
13. "I am helpless and have no control over what I feel."
14. "I never do anything right."
15. "Everyone looks down on me."
16. "I'll make a fool of myself."
17. "I'll fail."

For the purposes of discussion, we've found the most utility with the first eight self-limiting beliefs. It's important to try to get to the lowest common denominator or what lies beneath the other beliefs. Once students are aware of this from the experiences on their adventure-based course, it will be easier for them to detect when it emerges in other edge situations at the school, office, or home.

5. Conversation

The conversations we are referring to is the self-talk we have with ourselves. It has also been called the internal dialogue or the inner committee. This conversation often becomes the structure that supports and affirms our self-limiting beliefs. The beliefs then are similar to an architect's blueprints. The conversation is the building that is erected to match the plans. Even though the blueprint or belief may be erroneous, we still blindly build a case or a structure to support it. Without realizing it, we constantly talk to ourselves, either planning, confirming or disconfirming our map of the world.

It has been noted that people generally speak at an average of 150 words a minute. Yet, the inner dialogue occurs at a rate of 400 to 650 words per minute (Tracy, 1987). When someone is speaking to us, there is a tendency to fill in the spaces between their words with many of our own thoughts, which can lead to poor listening. For the sake of illustration, let's see how much we say to ourselves in one day. At the rate of 400 words a minute, that is 24,000 words in an hour or 384,000 words in a 16-hour day. If we break this up into seven-word sentences, we come up with a total of 54,857 sentences are communicated to ourselves on a daily basis. This is a staggering amount of reinforcement, which may be directed toward erroneous, irrational or outdated beliefs, which in turn can be overwhelming and difficult to interrupt.

We want to help students become aware of their internal dialogue and to learn how to challenge those statements that are debilitating. It is important for students to realize that when they get to the edge of the unknown, their conversations will most likely get louder and that their spoken words will influence other edge components like their physiology, metaphors, and feelings. Our bodies respond to our statements, even though they may not be true. In addition, the conversation will give clues to which beliefs are being overcompensated for or supported.

As an example, one student, Jim, frequently operated under the belief of "I can't." The conversation that supported this belief as he got close to the edge was, "I always mess up"; "I'll never be able to do this"; "People are going to laugh at me"; "This is too hard"; "No way"; "Maybe I'll refuse to do it." This all transpired in a few seconds and left him scared, resistant, and pessimistic about the activity. We were able to work with him on challenging some of these thoughts and talking about his "I can't" belief. He eventually changed some of his self-talk at the edge, which lessened his feelings of fear, and he broke through to new territory, where in the past he would have retreated.

6. Support

Support is an edge component that a person uses to get from the comfortable zone to new territory. It can be constructive or many times be something that is overused, destructive, or unhealthy. What was once effective as a strength can be overused and become a weakness, as it prevents the possibility for new actions. As leaders, we want to help students be aware of what they are using as support and allow them to make healthy choices.

A person's actions and choices are usually viewed as serving a positive intention for them. In some way, those individuals think the actions and choices are helpful. Most people will choose a support because it is either self-nurturing or self-protective, or both. Some qualities or components that make up a support system include: (a) consistency, (b) security, (c) safety, (d) tension relief, (e) nourishment, (f) trustworthiness, and (g) encouragement. In this light, you can see how a person may depend on alcohol, drugs, food, work, or a relationship to provide these qualities.

Let's look at a few examples. Dan was a 17-year-old adolescent on an adventure-based course. He had used alcohol since he was thirteen. In going to parties with his friends, he always drank before and during the party. He reported, "I liked the way I felt; it let me talk with people better." In other words, when approaching new territory, like a party or the opposite sex, there was safety, security, dependability, and trust in the alcohol that he could feel better. Plus, there was encouragement (Alcoholics Anonymous talks about the "bottle of courage"), nurturance, and tension relief in taking new risks, which without the alcohol, would have been more frightening. Dan used alcohol, where others in similar situations may have used drugs, food, work or a dependent relationship. While on a course, students, like Dan, have the opportunity to explore what means of support they used in the past and experiment with new constructive ways of asking for and getting support.

While on a corporate teambuilding program, the team had already discussed the three statements that don't get spoken in the corporate world, from Mark McCormack's *What They Still Don't Teach You at Harvard Business School* (1990). These are: (1) "I don't know," (2) "I made a mistake," and (3) "I need help." Mike, a manager, was in the middle of a group problem solving activity called the "acid river." He was blindfolded and really struggling to move across the board by himself. The instructor stopped him, while he was in this S-1 experience, and asked him what he was experiencing. He replied, "I'm frustrated." The instructor asked, "What do you need from others at this moment?" Mike said he didn't know. In spite of the instructor's persistence, the words "I need help" couldn't be pulled out of him, until another team member mentioned it. He then said, "Oh yeah, I need help." This request for help just wasn't a part of his repertoire. While debriefing, Mike became painfully aware of what it costs him, his staff, and his company when individuals don't know how to ask for and get help and support.

When students can experiment with new behaviors and ask for support while at the edge on a course, they will have a better chance of using new resources at the edge in the office, school, or at home. Some examples of positive supports that students can learn and carry home to use at the edge include:

1. A positive relationship with a friend, therapist, co-worker, boss, or sponsor, who encourages and supports without rescuing;
2. The ability to develop an inner "coach," "nurturing parent," or "wise sage";
3. Relaxation, meditation, exercise, or self-hypnosis that the individual can use at the edge to relax, recharge, and encourage;
4. Journal writing to help put the edge components into perspective;
5. 12-step programs;
6. A sense of a higher power, where they can feel support and guidance;
7. Support groups at work or in the community, where individuals can share apprehensions and fears and know it won't be used against them. Instead, they can experience the support and encouragement to stretch into new territories.

7. Metaphors

"I feel like a million dollars." "I'm on the top of the world." "My heart is beating like a race horse." "I can see the light at the end of the tunnel." Metaphors such as these are very effective in communicating an experience. They are widely accepted, spoken daily, and usually have unconscious roots. Siegelman (1990) stated that " . . . metaphor is primary both in language and in thought. It is through metaphor that language itself develops. . . . Metaphor is not just a figure of speech but an elementary structure of thought. . . . As the quintessential 'bridging operation', metaphor links domains by connecting insight and feeling, and what is known with what is only guessed at" (p. 3).

As students move into new territory, they have experiences that are "beyond words." The use of and facilitation for metaphors can help bring this unknown and unfamiliar experience into the known and familiar circle of comfort. Essentially, the metaphoric process entails describing one thing in terms of another and with this comparison a third thing the new idea, is born (Siegelman, 1990).

A metaphor is something that stands for something else. Making metaphors is a natural and sometimes unconscious process humans use in thinking and communicating. It may be a symbol like a word, object, painting, statue, gesture, or mental image. A metaphor may be expressed in a story or a song, or it could be a ceremony or ritual that holds symbolic importance for the people performing it. For our purposes, a metaphor encompasses all the linguistic and visual aspects we create and utilize as symbols or markers for our human existence. The story and pictures that describe the metaphor have a significant influence on both what we bring to the edge, along with what we create and take back from the new adventure. We have saved this component for last, because a person's metaphors at the edge can include and stand for all the other edge components. One picture can stand for 1,000 words at S-1.

Bateson said that a metaphor is "the pattern that connects" (Combs & Freedman, 1990, p. 16). He believed that metaphors were inescapable in living systems because every thought we have is about something. For example, when we think of a compass, we don't see the word, but instead we create a picture of an object that's a metaphor describing where north is located. Metaphors can be used to create patterns that connect the adventure-based experience with the office, school, or home environment. Therefore, we need to help students clarify and magnify the metaphors that they use to transfer and generalize the experience.

In actuality, students are unconsciously trying to connect or make sense of the experience. You can help them by making the process more conscious and thus transferable. This process is akin to, first, orienting the map so that it accurately represents the territory. That is helping students become aware of how they had a breakthrough and, second, imprinting this new map or picture on the brain so it can be quickly retrieved and utilized for breakthroughs when students are at new edges.

The American Memory Institute (1989) reports that memory is a series of pictures that we create and then recall. To improve memory, they advocate creating engaging and exciting pictures about things. We know on a course the day is full of exciting and engaging activities. Our task then is to help students connect or make conscious these pictures and have them stand for the specific learning that they have experienced. In other words, to turn their learning into graphic pictures or metaphors as a means of remembering and transferring the experience. This process is elaborated further in a subsequent section entitled, "Developing and Using Metaphors."

Metaphors at the Edge

When student are at the edge of new territory, they are embarking into a land of experiences and feelings that may be without words. A great deal may be going on for them unconsciously and influencing them without their awareness. The metaphor provides a window to the experience that becomes a transitional phenomenon linking one's inner experience and the outer world. Our task is to help make implicit metaphors explicit, so they become available for association, examination, and reworking.

Stopping the activity in S-1 will help to open the window to see what is inside. Without facilitating for a metaphor the success or retreat may happen quickly and unconsciously. The information of what prevented them from taking the risk or how they motivated themselves to "go for it" is lost, as is the learning and knowledge for transfer. As stated earlier, at the edge, the first objective is to help students become aware of what is going on. Inquiring about their physiology, feelings, patterns, conversations, beliefs, and support will help create a picture for them. Then we ask the questions, "What is an image that you see now?" "What pictures are you making in your mind now?" "If we videotaped you feeling and saying these things to yourself, what kind of picture would we see?" "What is it like to be where you are at this moment?"

Frequently, when a student is at the edge and scared or unsure, an old image may be activated. They may see themselves as the small child they once were, with foreboding or critical parents saying things to them. Now it's themselves who are repeating these statements, and feeling small as a consequence. This is the picture, of being and feeling small, that we want to evoke and make conscious.

Encouraging students to take the risk or change some of their edge components will help form the basis for alternative and more constructive metaphors. When they have had a success and are in S+1, you can ask, "What is that image like?"; "What is the picture or symbol?". This is important to identify so the students can carry the picture to other activities and home. It is something they can flash to when at a new edge but with old pictures. When students become conscious of this process, they begin to take charge of their personal slide show. The old image appears; they are aware of it, and replace this slide with the S+1 slide. Changing this metaphor can also change their affect, along with their physiology, beliefs, and internal conversations.

For example, after a ropes course initiative called the "trapeze leap," we worked with students to come up with metaphors for their experience. Some examples included: "a soaring eagle," "an angel with wings," "a person unshackled," and "someone lifted by the hand of God." These metaphors were then used in the processing of the experience and talk of transference. Statements like, "What does your eagle need to do to soar at work?" "How can you get unshackled when you're at home?" "If your angel with wings was with you at home, I wonder what successes you would have." When we talk metaphorically, the unconscious gets stimulated, which may help students make connections more easily, and in the end they become creators of empowering metaphors, rather than prisoners of outdated images.

Putting It All Together

Edgework is enhanced by using the levels of processing. Once at the edge, you can help students become aware of what they are saying, doing, thinking, feeling, and viewing. Then, you can focus on whether this is a typical or common pattern for the individual, so that the person can take responsibility. Students, in other words, own their patterns. They move from "I did?" in the awareness level to "I do!" in the responsibility level. Once that is established, you can encourage students to take some risks, experiment with new patterns, and do something different at the edge. Because the edge components influence each other and are interdependent, making a change in one component can alter the other components. Then, students can feel more empowered; that there are more choices for them and that they are not stuck.

The choice level is important for students. Here, they realize that they can choose to stay the same or make changes; it is totally up to them. Experimenting at the edge gives them information about what is possible, so they can make an informed choice. When risks or experiments are taken, the processing focuses on "What was it like for you?", "How did it work?", "How can we support you?", "What do you need to adjust?", etc. The group focus can be on the evaluation of the experiment, the outcomes, and what, if any, adjustments are needed to refine the experiment.

Below are some selected examples of edgework. The first column signifies the old pattern that has been owned at the edge while on the course, and the second column shows the new resources that the student is experimenting with at new edges—at the office, home, or school.

George was a 30-year-old manager for a small family-run business. The new territory for him was a promotion at the office, where he would have to manage 20 people and do more public speaking within the company and to future customers.

Old Edge Patterns	Edge Resources
Feelings: Scared and feeling sorry for self	*Feelings:* Satisfied and content
Physiology: Heart racing and losing breath	*Physiology:* Take deep breath and long, slow exhale
Pattern/Defense: Avoid, wait, hide, and people please	*Pattern/Defense:* Move forward, take the risk, and please self
Belief: "Something is wrong with me." "I don't know."	*Belief:* "I accept myself."
Conversation: "I may fail." "I may get rejected."	*Conversation:* "I'm not a bad person." "People like me."
Support: Overeat	*Support:* Friends, self, and group support
Metaphor: Pictures self on the outside of a circle of people as an "outcast."	*Metaphor:* Picture last success speaking at a meeting. Looks at receptive audience and sees face of woman who complimented him on his speech.

Elizabeth was a 59-year-old woman who has been in recovery from alcoholism for the last ten years. The new territory at home for her was living alone after the death of her husband and running her own business.

Old Edge Patterns	Edge Resources
Feelings: Scared and anxious	*Feelings:* Pride and satisfaction from successes
Physiology: Shallow breathing, holding arms over stomach, and bent posture	*Physiology:* Breathe deep, move arms off stomach, and sit tall
Pattern/Defense: Avoid situations	*Pattern/Defense:* Just do it without thinking
Belief: "Something is wrong with me" "I'm stupid."	*Belief:* "I can." "I'm okay the way I am."
Conversation: "This is too much for me." "I can't handle this."	*Conversation:* "I can handle it." "One step at a time."
Support: Husband Bottle (in the past)	*Support:* Asking for help, Alcoholics Anonymous, and pleasing self
Metaphor: Pictures self as scared child in the fetal position	*Metaphor:* Pictures successes as a capable and nurturing adult helping others

Greg was a 17-year-old in a treatment center for chemical dependency. The new territory for him was doing well in school and finding new friends and activities that didn't involve drugs and alcohol.

Old Edge Patterns	Edge Resources
Feelings: Fear, anger, pity	*Feelings:* Excitement and the joy of discovery
Physiology: Sighing, dropping head, and shallow breathing	*Physiology:* Sitting tall and taking deep breaths with long exhales
Pattern/Defense: Put things off and procrastinate	*Pattern/Defense:* Do it right now
Belief: "I can't." "I don't know."	*Belief:* "I can." "Just do my best."
Conversation: "It's too late." "I won't make it."	*Conversation:* "I'll never know unless I give it a try." "Do it anyway."
Support: Beer and cocaine	*Support:* Family, sponsor, Alcoholics Anonymous, and therapist
Metaphor: Pictures a person in a rut or on a bicycle just "spinning my wheels and going nowhere."	*Metaphor:* Pictures success of doing a long rappel in spite of his fear.

In summary, the adventure-based experience or any new learning event can put individuals at the edge of new territory. This is where it appears to be unfamiliar, unknown, and unpredictable. There are feelings of discomfort, disequilibrium, and risk. The person either retreats or withdraws from this edge or "goes for it" and may have a breakthrough or a success. Edgework puts this moment at the edge under the microscope and examines the components. Old and outdated edge patterns are recognized and altered or discarded in favor of trying some new behaviors, thoughts, and feelings. These new actions or resources can then become the gems to treasure, transfer, and generalize the experience to the new territories of the office, home, or school.

Corrective Emotional Experience

In a story told by psychotherapist, Paul Watzlawick (1990), a man persisted in clapping his hands to keep the elephants away from him. A therapist tried in vain to explain to the man that there were no elephants. The man quickly responded, "You see." He assumed his solution was working. Watzlawick (1990) explains that there are four ways to try and change this man's phobia. They are:

1. In a trusting relationship with a professional or friend, convincing the man there were no elephants.

2. Using insight as the agent of change. Here the unconscious motivations for this fear would be examined and brought into consciousness, which would then help him let go of this symptom.

3. Bring an elephant into the therapy session and to show that clapping his hands doesn't work to keep the elephant away.

4. The man breaks his wrist and can't clap. He sees then that the elephants haven't charged him, and maybe it wasn't the clapping that kept them away.

During an adventure-based course, we typically use all four of these approaches to help students deal with their fears at the edge. The fourth approach is a life experience that happens in an unplanned random manner. This doesn't happen frequently on a course, yet there are time that you may have observed when a random event (severe storm), a mistake (getting lost), or crisis (first aid emergency) provided an opportunity for significant learning to occur for a student or the group. In many of those instances the growth that occurred as a result of the experience couldn't have turned out better if it was planned.

Given the value of significant unplanned learning, Watzlawick (1990) advocates creating what he calls "planned chance events" to bring about change. In this section, we will discuss these four ways of creating change and explore the "corrective emotional experience" that occurs on a course directly and sometimes indirectly.

The term "corrective emotional experience", which was coined by Franz Alexander (1946), who studied how people change, aptly describes what experiential learning provides for students. The experience is "affectively" loaded and in many cases is corrective for an individual. In other words, we help students "change the viewing" and "change the doing" of the problem (O'Hanlon, 1990). Students' perceptions of the problem may change, and as a result, they act or interact differently in relation to the problem. There are two types of corrective emotional experiences: (1) the therapeutic relationship, and (2) new experiences in life.

Therapeutic Relationship

For our purpose, we will call both the relationship that exists between the student and the instructor and the relationships that are developed among the group members, therapeutic. There has been much written about the curative factors of a group (Yalom, 1985). A few points that are relevant to this discussion are (1) the sense of universality—all the members of the group see how their concerns are similar to those of others, (2) group cohesiveness—the sense of connection and good feelings when the group works together well, (3) improved interpersonal communication—members feel listened to and understood, and (4) the recapitulation of the family unit—this encompasses the reparenting that transpires within a group.

Support is important for students to experience so they can take new risks. This is similar to the recapitulation of the family unit. Our students unconsciously are wondering if the course or experiences are safe and if it is okay to trust others. Can they gingerly move into new territory and explore, without the fear of criticism or rejection? Early experiences in the family, usually with the mother, may become reactivated. If it was hard for the student to trust his mother for safety and security, the leader may see a reticent and anxious student. In turn, if exploration as a child was prohibited, taking new risks on a course may feel frightening. Therefore, early in the course, you are encouraged to establish a safe and supportive environment within the group. This foundation established the groundwork for new risks to be taken.

Corrective emotional experience ingredients for developing trust and encouragement include the following:

1. **Trust Phase:**
    a. Permission to feel and be
    b. Safety and security
    c. Consistency
    d. Empathy and support
2. **Encouragement Phase:**
    a. Encouragement to explore and take risks
    b. Affirming individuality
    c. Failure is necessary step for success
    d. Support for person rather than the performance
    e. Encouragement to ask for help and support

Winnicott (1985) proposed the term "holding environment" as a metaphor for the total protective, empathic care that the "good enough" mother provides the infant during the first few years of life. You have a challenging responsibility in creating this "holding environment." Adjusting to the "ever-shifting needs" of one person is difficult, let alone adjust to 10 to 12 students' "fluctuating needs." You may be encouraging one student to take a risk, while comforting another who requires less tension and more soothing and trust building. This is where maintaining the constructive level of anxiety, which is different for each student, demands attention to and understanding of the specific capacities and needs of each student in your group.

New Experiences

Providing new experiences as part of the corrective emotional experience may be the primary factor which promotes the significant learning, growth, and changes that are evident during adventure-based learning experiences. As expressed earlier, many educational theorists emphasize the value of new experiences or action. Gregory Bateson argued that new and different experiences are essential for personal growth. He suggested that all information is necessarily ''news of difference,'' and that it is the perception of difference that triggers all new responses in living systems (White & Epston, 1990). Jean Piaget (1954) in his book entitled *The Construction of Reality in the Child*, contends that children literally construct their reality by exploring actions, rather than first forming an image of the world through their perceptions and then beginning to act accordingly. If Piaget's perspective is accurate then we would assume that different actions may lead to the construction of different realities.

Figure 18. Rappeling: A New Experience for Course Participants

A similar view was suggested by Milton Erickson (1948), who believed that experience was the best teacher. As a result, he was a therapist who attempted to design experiences that allowed people to reach their goals. He wrote: "It is the experience of reassociating and reorganizing his own experiential life that eventuates in a cure. . . . The patient's task is that of learning through his own efforts to understand his experiential life in a new way (1948, p. 38–39).

There are an abundance of activities and experiences that comprise an adventure-based course, most of which are new for students. Therefore, it is likely that at least one activity will be the planned chance event that provides a "change of viewing" or a "change of doing." Processing can be viewed as a coding mechanism. When the new experience is coded, it then can be more easily generalized and applied to the office, school, or home. Consequently, you want to first get students to try something different and, second, process or codify the experience to establish exactly what was different; then this experience can be utilized in the future.

At the beginning of this section we shared a story about the man and the elephant. No amount of insight or explaining, even within a trusting relationship, could alter this man's reality as much as the action of breaking his wrist or being with the elephant and seeing his hand clapping didn't work. Each of these provided a new experience which had to be integrated into his conscious knowing. One is an example of a direct new experience, and the other an indirect new experience.

Direct new experiences can be facilitated by using the levels of processing format. When students become aware and responsible for their edge components, then they can be encouraged to take new risks. This gives them an opportunity to create a new reality for themselves. They can have a breakthrough or success and expand their circle of comfort or sense of competency. This is a direct new experience in that they are fully responsible for taking the actions.

As previously mentioned, taking any new action on an edge component can alter the other components and help propel them into new territory. Support and encouragement to experiment with new behaviors and facilitation about the experimentation then becomes the main task for leaders. It is through these steps that students are helped to evaluate their experiences and construct personal meaning from them.

Planned Chance Events

Planned chance events refer to indirect experiences that the student hasn't actually self-selected, yet which occur because they have agreed to participate on the course. Usually these indirect experiences are structured by the instructor. Other times, they may come from random events. They are "planned" in that you may think this experience will benefit the students by helping them stretch to new areas where they may not have gone on their own. Leaders have always done this, designed an activity in a creative way. Here we are encouraging you to consider this kind of intervention more as a means of giving students breakthrough experience. You can be very creative in generating "planned chance events." The more personal risks that you can take within the scope of good judgement (never compromising safety), the more successes you and your students can have.

An example from an adventure-based program for adjudicated youths may be appropriate at this point. The students had been in the field for ten days of a 19-day course. There has been several incidents of stolen food, usually the cookies, without the thieves identifying themselves or being caught. The instructor decided to approach the issue in an indirect way. He sent the crew out to collect firewood. While they were away from camp, he stole the fudge cookies from one of the student's backpacks. After dinner, the group was anxiously awaiting their treats. When the student couldn't find the cookies, a group meeting was called. All the students were angry and upset about this. An excellent discussion ensued about trust, feeling violated, and honesty. Even the suspected thieves got involved and shared pertinent feelings. The instructor then pulled out the cookies. After some initial shock and resentment, the students all responded how that it had been a great learning experience. Obviously, this planned chance event was risky and took time to plan and implement, but the outcome was very fruitful. Students were compelled to go outside their circle of comfort and discuss personal matters of significance.

One way to set up planned chance events is to use handicaps; where one sense is taken away during an activity (see Using Handicaps section, pages 89 to 91 for some further ideas). While handicapped students are thrust to their edge, feeling a constructive level of anxiety, something unique or significant may occur. You may not know what the student will experience, but you need to trust in the student's ability to learn from being impelled into the new territory. In addition to using handicaps with students, you can use any of the following suggestions to bring about planned chance events:

1. Encouraging students to try out opposite roles than they normally take.

2. Designing activities and discussions at unusual times, i.e., night or early morning.

3. Selecting specific students to be leaders, followers, a person sabotaging the experience or a complainer (especially if this what the person typically does; this is called ''prescribing the symptom''). Or be the worst leader you can be in the next activity. Usually, the more absurd or unique it sounds, the more potential there is for breakthroughs.

4. Making note of and emphasizing the smallest changes that are observed and which are probably seen as only random events by students.

New experiences, then, whether direct or initiated by the student's experimentation or indirect and suggested or designed by the leader, are a major force in moving students into new territory. Once in new territory, the processing of the experience is what gives the new learning meaning for the student to bring back to the office, home, or school. As a result, the new territory is tamed, and the adventure-based experience can become a corrective emotional experience. The students may add a significant chapter of successes and increased self-efficacy to their life stories. Their unique outcomes, then, can be plotted in an alternative story, which then can alter their lives and their relationships.

Feelings Aren't Biodegradable

People frequently have a misunderstanding about the way that litter biodegrades when left in wilderness areas. This misconception also applies to how we deal with our feelings. That is, many people believe that if painful or uncomfortable feelings are left unattended, they will magically disappear. This section explores these misconceptions and describes some interventions that can be undertaken to positively deal with feelings.

In the wilderness, many individual have a difficult time with the concept of biodegradable. Most of us have observed students throwing orange peels or apples cores into the woods and when asked about their behavior, they respond, "They're biodegradable." Students also bathe upstream from where people are cooking and when asked about the soap in the water they respond "It's Dr. Bronner's soap, and it's biodegradable." It seems that there's a magical quality given to the term biodegradable which somehow indicates that instantly peels, apple cores, or soap will decompose or dissolve.

The Oxford Dictionary (1990) defines biodegradable as "capable of being decomposed by bacteria or other living organisms" (p. 109). Degrade is defined as "1) to diminish with deteriorating effect; 2) To break up into small lumps or into dust; 3) To reduce the strength of—giving a tendency to deteriorate or disintegrate . . ." (p. 367). What is often misunderstood by students is the time or duration that is involved in this deterioration process. During this process, the substance is a contaminate that alters the ecology. Some examples of the length of biodegradation cited in the *Instructor's Field Manual, North Carolina Outward Bound School,* (1980) are:

Aluminum cans:	80–100 years
Nylon fabrics:	30–40 years
Paper containers with plastic coating:	5 years
Paper containers:	2 weeks to 5 months
Fecal matter:	1–4 weeks
Orange peels:	1 week to 6 months

In a similar manner, unresolved feelings are a contaminate to the human system. Even though the feelings are hidden or repressed, individuals are influenced, at times burdened, or even imprisoned by them. The impact of these feelings usually occurs unconsciously since individuals are not aware that their toxin is seeping through in unrecognizable ways.

Because feelings are hidden we often think that others won't see them. Yet, we have all met people who later we wondered: "Why is he mad at the world?" or "What's her problem?". A maxim from Alcoholics Anonymous is that "Whenever you bury a feeling, you bury it alive." It may grow in unexpected and unwanted ways.

Generally speaking, people don't know what to do with their feelings. They can be painful, uncomfortable, and embarrassing. So, why not just ignore them or run away from them? Our society promotes this. We've all received "don't feel" messages, such as:

"Be strong, will you?"

"Big boys don't cry."

"Come on now; you'll get over it."

"You are always so sensitive."

"You are just too emotional."

"It's not that big a deal."

"Why are you always crying about everything?"

"Just do this (instead of feeling)."

"Tomorrow you won't think twice about this."

"Don't let them see you sweat."

And even, "Don't worry; be happy."

While these messages are verbal, there are also many non-verbal messages to not feel, create waves, or burden others with your feelings. The ideal of the perfect family, where there aren't problems or arguments fosters this repression of feelings. Television promotes "don't feel" messages with commercials to self-medicate anytime you feel slightly uncomfortable. Contac, Anacin, Excedrin, Scope, Tums, Alka Seltzer, and Rolaids will all help you to not feel. Researchers have noted that 80% of people who see medical doctors do so for lifestyle or emotional reasons. And how are most of these problems taken care of? By being given some type of medication to correct their feelings. Accordingly, it is not a surprise that most people think that feelings will somehow just biodegrade if we don't attend to them and just ignore them. We are never taught in school or from most parents how to learn from feelings or what to do with them. Instead we learn how to avoid or stuff feelings.

There are some feelings that are more difficult and painful than others to experience. These feelings are the deep emotions which all of us have, but most likely hide. We hide them with our defenses, which were mentioned earlier. Also, we hide these deeper feelings with surface feelings which are easier to experience and which distract us from deeper feelings (see figure 19). The middle layer feelings also protect the deep feelings from being revealed or acknowledged. These deeper feelings are the ones that don't biodegrade, unless they are given attention. They can endure, like the aluminum can in the wilderness, for a lifetime. All that time they are negatively impacting our system, although observable through attitudes, defenses, surface feelings, metaphoric language, and psychosomatic illnesses.

An example may help elucidate this process. Jim, a student on an 8-day course, was a sexist and chauvinist. He was often angry or depressed. Underneath these surface feelings he revealed an experience that housed his deeper feelings. Jim had been married for four years in what he thought was a good relationship. One day he came home and

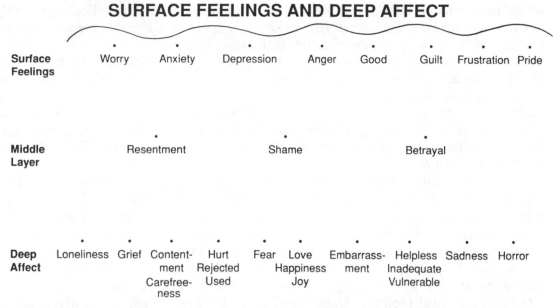

SURFACE FEELINGS AND DEEP AFFECT

Surface Feelings	Worry	Anxiety	Depression	Anger	Good	Guilt	Frustration	Pride

Middle Layer	Resentment	Shame	Betrayal

Deep Affect	Loneliness	Grief	Content-ment / Carefree-ness	Hurt / Rejected / Used	Fear	Love / Happiness / Joy	Embarrass-ment	Helpless / Inadequate / Vulnerable	Sadness	Horror

Figure 19. Surface Feelings and Deep Affect (Adapted from Fabian et al. 1985)

found his wife in bed with another man. He left that night, never to see his wife again. His obvious feelings of rejection, hurt, embarrassment, grief, helplessness, and horror were all present but avoided. In the subsequent years, the contamination from the non-biodegradable emotions exhibited themselves by treating other women horribly, being obnoxious, angry, and becoming addicted to cocaine and alcohol. In talking about his ex-wife 12 years later, the anger and deeper feelings of hurt and rejection were present, as if the incident had happened the week before, a strong indication that his unacknowledged and avoided deeper feelings did not biodegrade. By sharing his true feelings, he was more accepted and understood by others as a result of revealing his "secret." He began to realize that he wasn't as horrible and worthless as he had thought; rather that he was just hurt and rejected and that he could be understood and accepted by others. His deeper feelings were able to change after being released.

What to Do with Feelings

As mentioned earlier, many of us "HIDe" our deeper feelings. We haven't learned how to constructively deal with and manage feelings. A beneficial change would be to allow feelings that have been HID to surface. To do this, we can change HID to the acronym IHD. This stands for (1) *I*dentify and acknowledge feelings, (2) *H*onor and accept the feelings, and (3) *D*eliver, experience, or communicate the feelings to yourself, another, or the source. The following is a more extensive explanation of each of these steps:

1. **Identify and Acknowledge Feelings:** First, you need to know the aluminum can doesn't belong in the wilderness and is a pollutant to the environment. With feelings, some of this knowledge is imparted by education that feelings are a significant part of the human experience, just like the wind, rain, and animals are a part of the wilderness experience. With feelings, some of this knowledge is imparted by education that feelings are a significant part of the human experience, just like the

wind, rain, and animals are a part of the wilderness experience. Feelings aren't right or wrong; they are part of life and exist in their own right. Experiencing our feelings helps get through them, rather than avoiding them.

We ride out storms in the wilderness and work at getting comfortable in those uncomfortable situations. Putting extra clothes on or sitting under a tarp helps us get through storms. We usually realize it's foolish to run from every storm. We learn to navigate through and manage the elements, and usually feel more capable after weathering the storm. The next storm usually is less threatening. Feelings, like storms, come in waves of intensity followed by the quiet peacefulness that exists after the storm.

We can usually observe signs that inclement weather is on its way, which is similar to the existence of signs to identify that deeper feelings are in the air. Some typical signs are (a) Surface feelings—usually under each of these surface feelings hides a deeper and more painful emotion. The surface feelings can begin or end abruptly or last for days. Their chief goal is to maintain the status quo. People who are always laughing or smiling inappropriately usually will tell you that they would cry if they weren't laughing. Often, the depressed person is moving away from more painful feelings. Underneath anger towards others is usually anger at oneself or a significant other. Anxiety may be blocking a fear of rejection or of being hurt. (b) Psychosomatic signs—often betray some deeper feelings. Headaches, migraines, nervous stomach, cracking voice, sweaty palms, dizziness, all may be indications that some deeper affects are being activated (see nonverbal behavior and communication on pages 29 to 31). (c) Defenses—such as intellectualizing, blaming others, charming people, being the clown, the know-it-all, the airhead, and the perfect student are all roles that protect the more sensitive and vulnerable feelings. (d) Metaphors—are descriptive means to describe painful experiences. Examples include: ''I have a lump in my throat''; ''My heart is racing''; ''I feel dead inside''; ''There's an emptiness or hollowness within me''; ''I have a knot in my chest''; ''It's like having your arms cut off''; ''It was like a slap in the face to me''; ''It was like I was bleeding to death and no one cared.'' These metaphors are very graphic. They powerfully describe the deeper feelings that may be imprisoned and inexpressible. Often these feelings occurred early in life and are communicated in the words of a child.

These types of signs can give you information about the students that you are working with. By noting the external behaviors and communicating them to students, you can help them identify and acknowledge their feelings. The awareness questions found in the levels of processing section also can be used to facilitate the identification of feelings.

2. **Honor and Accept the Feelings:** After we have identified the feeling, we want to honor it. Here students are encouraged to accept and own their feelings as being valuable components in the human system. In the ecological system, storms and rain are integral for the continued growth of the environment. At this stage of the process the message of ''It's okay to feel'' seeks to take the place of the conditioned ''Don't feel'' messages. Honoring one's feelings is a means of owning or being responsible for this emotional domain. It is a way to be true to yourself. At times it may be appropriate to surrender to the feeling rather than fighting it. This is similar to surrendering to a storm and altering your travel plans.

People feel all the time, in differing intensity levels. Every feeling brings information about who we really are at that moment. In an effort to honor feelings, Fabian (1984) suggests that we avoid spending time doing the following:

1. Needing to explain them or find a reason for them.
2. Searching for their source or unearthing their cause.
3. Finding out what they mean.
4. "Doing something" about them or "getting something done" about them.
5. Enduring them as a kind of martyrdom.
6. Forcing deep affect into awareness. Rather, we need to take deep feelings as they come.

Others in our life don't help in honoring our feelings when they want to become Mr. or Mrs. Fixit. Instead, we need encouragement to feel our feelings and believe that "We'll handle it" or weather this storm. So, once our feelings are identified, then we honor their existence or become honest with ourselves that we have them, in spite of the fact that they may not feel good. In the wilderness, we first notice the aluminum can and by realizing the can is polluting or contaminating the environment, we are honoring the ecology and thus becoming aware that something must be done with this toxin. To feel is natural; to avoid feelings is unnatural and presents a dam in the natural flow of emotions.

3. **Deliver, Experience or Communicate the Feelings to Yourself, Another, or the Source:** In this stage we retrieve the aluminum can, put it in our backpack, and carry it out. Similarly, our feelings are retrieved, experienced, and carried out. There are times when a person is truly experiencing their deep affects and no words need to be expressed. A shift has occurred. The emotion is felt and thus delivered between two individuals. It can be a look, shared sentiment, hand on the shoulder, or other nonverbal communication.

Many times, though, more of an effort is needed to deliver these emotions. This may entail communication of these feelings to others or the source with whom the feelings were experienced. Expressing feelings in a responsible manner with I-statements is appropriate. Defensiveness or blaming doesn't allow the deeper affect to be delivered. Ideally, the leader will teach and role model how to express deeper feelings, while creating a safe environment within the group to make this possible. Practicing this process in the group can be very beneficial. Role playing a significant other in the group or at home can also help.

If a person that you feel comfortable with or the source of these feelings is unavailable, expressing them to yourself via journal writing can be very effective. The act of experiencing and communicating deep feelings using any available mode can be very healing in itself. This provides an opportunity to let go, which in turn can create more energy for dealing with here and now relationships.

One of the fears commonly experienced by individuals in regard to dealing with their feelings is that if they really sample this forbidden feeling, it will overwhelm them and never stop. This is untrue. Feelings are like waves that have moments of intensity, then dissipate and come back in a wave. Students need to understand this in order to give themselves permission to feel. In most cases, a student will remain at a heightened emotional state for less than ten minutes, and there will always be intermissions. When feelings are truly felt and experienced, there is a change or shift. Fabian (1984) stated that ". . . everyone's storehouse of difficult deep emotions is FINITE. That is, people who persist in facing their difficult deep emotions will, within a period of months, finish the job!" (p. 2).

On adventure-based courses, students will engage in activities where deeper feelings are activated or elicited. This is an opportunity for students to learn how to express and feel these feelings. This is a new skill for many students, like rock climbing or rappelling, and they need to become comfortable with their emotions. As expressed in the foreword, you are not expected to do psychotherapy. If you don't have the necessary skills or training, don't try to deal with issues that you are uncomfortable with. However, the IHD process of identifying and acknowledging feelings, honoring the feelings, and then delivering the feelings appropriately can be a resource that students can utilize at home.

In summary, most of us have never learned how to deal with feelings constructively. We think these unresolved feelings are biodegradable, when in reality they are contaminating us like a toxin. What we have learned to do with feelings is:

Hold it in—Hold others off—Hold on

This is how the contaminate spreads. Now we can assist our students in navigating these negative emotions, by learning how to:

Let it out —Let others in—Let go

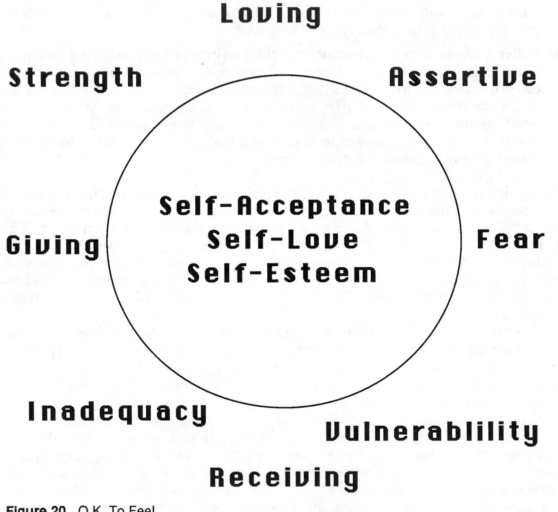

Figure 20. O.K. To Feel

86

A summary of what to do with feelings is found below:

Most of us have **HID** feelings and instead we want to use the **IHD PROCESS.**

I 1. **IDENTIFY AND ACKNOWLEDGE FEELINGS:**
"What are you feeling?"
Stay with feelings rather than stuff or avoid.
Look for the deeper emotions.

TYPICAL SIGNS INCLUDE:
A. Surface feelings   C. Defenses
B. Psychosomatic symptoms   D. Metaphors

H 2. **HONOR AND ACCEPT FEELINGS:**
"It's okay to feel."
"To heal you must feel."
No need to explain or unearth cause.
Ride with and through deep affect, as they come in waves.

D 3. **DELIVER, EXPERIENCE OR COMMUNICATE FEELINGS TO SELF OR OTHERS**
I statements, "I feel . . ."
When expressed, feelings will shift or change.
Moments of intensity are limited.
"You'll handle it."

Using Handicaps

Handicaps are challenges or tasks given to participants that take away one or more of their senses or abilities. The handicaps are usually unfamiliar and unexpected and, as a result, raise the level of disequilibrium in participants and the group. This disorientation can facilitate the restructuring of individuals' cognitive maps.

You can use handicaps at any time or with any event. The educational and therapeutic uses are unlimited. Deciding who, what handicap, which event and at what point in the event to use handicaps creates endless possibilities. It's important to know the individuals well, so the handicap creates a constructive level of anxiety and not a destructive one. Stretching of the limits is vital, as is trying to ensure success for the individual and group. If the level of anxiety becomes too high, you should consider removing the handicap. Handicaps can be used to make events more challenging for the individual, such as being blindfolded while climbing, or for the group, like doing an initiative with everyone non-verbal.

Another reason to use handicaps is to help individuals expand their potential. They are unable to rely solely on their strengths, like being verbal, being a leader, or using their physical power. The disequilibrium caused by handicaps compels participants to develop other abilities. When using handicaps, processing the experience is extremely important in order to raise individuals' levels of awareness, responsibility, and increase the possibility of transferring the learning home, to school or to the office.

Below is a list of some of the common handicaps that can be used and issues or themes to be gleaned when processing:

1. *Blind*—Participants are given a blindfold to put over their eyes. *Issues:* Powerlessness, being out of control, trust in others or a higher power, sense of the unknown or unexpected, and use of new senses or ways of knowing. What are you blind to in your future or recovery? This handicap is particularly well suited for individuals in recovery from chemical dependency.

2. *Nonverbal*—Participants are unable to speak to others. This is good to use with a leader or take-charge type person. *Issues:* Powerlessness, communicating in new ways, reliance on others, awareness of new senses, and being in new roles. A question to ask may be "What things in your life are you speechless about?"

3. *Paralyzed*—Participants are unable to use one of their arms or legs. This is good to use with someone who relies on their physical strength. *Issues:* Disabilities, powerlessness, reliance on body versus mind, feeling like a victim, dependency, teamwork, sense of the unexpected, and vulnerabilities. A question to ask may be, "What paralyzes you in work, relationships, or life?"

4. *Siamesed*—Participants are hooked together at the side like Siamese twins and must move together without any individual getting between them. This is good handicap to use in couple or family work. *Issues:* Compatibility, dependency on others, cooperation, enmeshment, consequence of how one affects the other and

Figure 21. Blindfolded on the Trolleys

commitment. This handicap can be used to get a passive and unengaged person involved when siamesed to an active leader type. A question to ask may be, "What issues are you and another stuck on?"

5. *Singled Voice*—Participants can only talk through another person. Somebody else is their voice, and they can only share ideas with this person who will then vocalize the idea to the whole group. This handicap, like the one above, is a good way to get a quiet person involved by sharing ideas of a leader with their voice. Couples and families are well suited for this handicap as well. Also, it can be used with bosses and employees, where the boss has to share the employee's ideas. *Issues:* Communication, listening, cooperation, not being heard, and being a leader. How does it feel to only share other's ideas and not your own? A question to ask may be, "What do you really want to say to others in your life?"

6. *Questions*—Participants are asked only to ask questions rather than make statements. This is good when some individuals are dominating the process, but you don't want to take their voice away. It lets them stay involved but in a challenging manner. *Issues:* Communication, dominance, the importance of clear communication, and cooperation. Questions to ask include "What was this like for you?" and "Who in your life do you need to ask more questions of, rather than making statements?"

7. *Killer and Suicide Statements*—Killer statements are ones like: "This won't work."; "That's a dumb idea."; while suicide statements are ones like: "I can't do this," "I'll never get over the wall." One or two participants are asked to make either of these statements to observe the effect on the group process. It's good to let it go for only five to ten minutes and then stop the group and ask them what they noticed. *Issues:* Negative forces within the group. People avoiding offering their ideas because they are afraid they'll get rejected. Questions to ask include:

"What happened to the team spirit when these statements were introduced?"
"Who makes killer and suicide statements in your life?"

8. **Confusion Technique**—Participants are asked to say the opposite of what someone else says. Usually one or two people are asked to assume this handicap. One member says "stop and go right.", the handicapped member says "let's go and go left." *Issues:* Opposition in the group, people talking at same time, poor communication, and inability to resolve conflict. Questions include: "How did the group experience this confusion?" "Where in your life do you get mixed messages and become confused?"

9. **Prescribing the Symptom**—A participant or two is asked to do the role he or she normally plays, especially when it's an unproductive role. Prescribing the symptom makes them conscious of what they are doing and what effect it may have on the other group members. *Issues:* Unproductive group role and raising awareness of the group process. Questions may include: "What effect does this role have on the group process?" "How does it feel to take this role?" "What do you think a person with this role gets out of it?"

Developing and Using Metaphors

Using metaphors has become very popular in the psychotherapy and mental health field. It appears that the use of metaphors is becoming a bridge between various psychological disciplines. Recently, there have been many publications written on using metaphorical communication (i.e., Combs & Freedman, 1990; Grove, 1989; Siegelman, 1990; White & Epston, 1990). This section will look closely at some of this work, plus give some practical suggestions on how you can use metaphorical communication with your students. The section is divided into three segments: (1) Using Students' Metaphors; (2) Leaders Using Metaphorical Communication; and (3) Creating Metaphors for Experiences and Feelings

Using Students' Metaphors

It is important to train your ears to recognize students' metaphors and then try to incorporate these metaphors in your responses. Using students' metaphors will help students know they have been heard and honored. People have a special relationship with their metaphors or stories, like they do with their names. We know communication can be enhanced when we use the person's name. The same is true for metaphors. The success of storying experiences provides persons with a sense of continuity and meaning in their lives, and they rely upon this for the ordering of daily lives and for the interpretation of further experiences (Combs & Freedman, 1990).

All stories have a beginning, middle, and ending or a history, present, and future. So, students' interpretations of current experiences is as much future-shaped as it is past-determined. It is in knowing and understanding the students' stories that we can help process their new experiences. Ask yourself how this new success can fit into the existing theme. You can help students rewrite their scripts as a director or producer would, understanding that reordering and changing the script, as a result of some disequilibrium, is very difficult and disturbing for some writers. The dominant story of the student is contained within the comfort and known circle. Being at the edge and into new territory creates new stories and metaphors that will take time to be accepted, so the dominant story can expand. New chapters or choices in life are then the result. The art of processing the experience is the means to bring about a richer story for the student, which can have broad appeal and application at home.

Having students tell their stories helps create the story. If it's untold or not put together well, only bits and fragments will exist. This point reinforces the suggestion of stopping students while they are in S-1. The edge components can then be exposed and included in the story so as to shed light on the retreat or the success. In S+1, the telling

93

of the story helps construct the full meaning of the experience. Bruner (1988) believes that in telling the story there is an opportunity to be in the experience again and create new meanings. He states that "It is in the performance of an expression that we re-experience, re-live, re-create, re-tell, re-construct, and re-fashion our culture. The performance does not release a pre-existing meaning that lies dormant in the text. . . . Rather, the performance itself is constitutive" (p. 11).

Some examples of using students' stories or metaphors will help illustrate this process. Nancy was a woman in her mid-thirties, and she spoke about feeling like she "was in a barrel and barely peeking over the edge" when she was in new situations. We talked about the barrel and gave feedback to her, like, "It seems like you came out of the barrel during the last activity. What was that like for you?" Jane was a woman in her sixties and spoke about a "knot" in her stomach when she felt her pain and loneliness. We continued to explore her "knot" with her during the course, i.e., "Is your knot there now? How big is it? What do you imagine your knot would like to do?" Jim was a 34-year-old man, who said, "Each time I achieve a new success at work, it's like grabbing an ice cube above me, and by the time I bring it down, it's melted, and I have to look for another." We talked with him about how he could savor this "ice cube" or success longer, before it melts. He decided to "treat it more like a treasure and keep it in an ice box with a window where I could view it and use it as a trophy to propel me further." Dan was a 48-year-old man who worked in a flower orchard for the past ten years. We talked to him about "pinching back the old growth when it gets in the way," listening to others as "fertilizing his soil", when he'd withdraw as "a freeze outside and all the flowers are closing up", and when he risked into new territory "as the emergence of a new petal unfolding."

After completing the ropes course, Susan, who was 28 years old and in recovery, talked about feeling like an "agile cat." We continued to speak to her about using "her balance of a cat" in other aspects of her life. "What would your cat do when things get shaky?" She responded "hold on tighter, like I have to do with my program and keep showing up; then, I know I'll always land on my feet."

In all these cases, we either used their metaphor or an aspect of their life story and utilized it as a symbol and means to enhance the communication and processing. The metaphor or story tells you the type of boat that they are navigating down the stream of their lives. We then jump in with them and use their specific language to help improve their steering and propulsion, so that they can arrive at new territories, landings, or choices in their lives.

Leaders Using Metaphorical Communication

When you use metaphorical communication, there is always an element of ambiguity in it. There are a number of ways it may be interpreted. People tend to want to resolve ambiguity, because it creates disequilibrium; thus more balance and stability are desired. Students will listen closer, think harder, and become more experientially involved when you use a certain amount of ambiguity when communicating information that is not safety related. Finding oneself in the unknown new territory can lead to a very active kind of participation where students are reassociating and reorganizing their internal experiential lives to find some order.

A metaphor or story is a nonlinear, indirect way of communicating. It encourages the student to be more actively mentally involved than direct communication. The individual must search through a number of stored or imagined experiences in order to find

Figure 22. "Cruising" Up a Rock Face

some personal meaning in a general symbol or story. The searching stimulates mental associations which make the communication more memorable. The creative process involved in searching through and reorganizing new experiences helps students become active collaborators in processing and generalizing their learning (Combs & Freedman, 1990).

In school, when a teacher stated, "If you don't all be quiet, some of you will stay after," it was easy to take this indirection as pointing a direct finger. Milton Erickson, the famous hypnotherapist, was renowned for using metaphors and indirection with his patients. He frequently told his patients to climb a nearby peak where they would learn something significant. Typically, they would come down with a profound experience, discovering why he sent them there. He used these experiences metaphorically, allowing his patients to come back with whatever learning they needed.

As a means of briefing an activity, you can use metaphors and indirection. Below are some examples:

1. "A student on the last course discovered an important personal strength on this next activity."

2. "Some of you may learn some significant things about yourselves today."

3. "Leadership can emerge from unexpected places."

4. "Don't be surprised when something extraordinary happens to you."

5. "I think many of you will really get what you came for from this activity (or course)."

When students are on the edge, the natural inclination is to move back into the circle of comfort; it's similar to a magnet pulling them. To combat this, you may need to encourage people unconsciously and indirectly, in addition to doing it directly. Metaphors can help with this process. Since ideas are not presented directly, it is more difficult for individuals to object to them (Combs & Freedman, 1990). The use of unconscious and indirect encouragement can help individuals to take those big steps and have the breakthroughs and successes they want.

Reverse Symbolism

People who have been involved in adventure-based education personally know the impact, potency, and learning that occurs from a course or program. It is possible that one of the major factors for this growth and relevancy comes from a process referred to as "reverse symbolism." That is, in almost all other educational situations, a learning, insight, or meaning is connected with a lived or real experience that acts as a symbol. For example, an educator may say to a student or friend "learning to use a computer is like riding a bicycle; you have to take many falls before you really get your balance and can go some distance" or "getting an advanced degree is like climbing a mountain; you just keep walking one step at a time." We take a concept or meaning and try to match it with a lived, active, or real symbol.

In adventure-based programs, we have the unique opportunity of engaging people in diverse real, active, and lived experiences. Reverse symbolism is one of the skills of processing where these lived or real experiences are taken as symbols and matched or connected with personal meanings for the individual. So, the symbolic or metaphoric experience goes from real life experience to meaning, where typically the analogy goes from meaning to a similar experience. If reverse symbolism doesn't take place, the activity stands as an unconnected, irrelevant, and unorganized experience for the person. When the experience is bridged with personal meaning for the individual, then the third thing created is the experience as a metaphor which can then stand for the learning and be used in an abundance of ways and situations. The reverse symbolism helps organize this new chapter within the dominant story for the person and becomes a valuable and useful resource. The experience becomes a symbol which is the golden nugget that now has value and can be exchanged, bought, and sold.

We have already established that our minds think in metaphorical or associative ways. In processing activities, instructors need only ask the right questions to facilitate what is a natural human process, making connections. When leaders use metaphorical communication, students are compelled to think and listen in symbols and will learn to make bridges from the experience to their life.

The direct and traditional way of processing may be to ask the question, "What did you learn about this experience that you can apply at home?" This approach beckons linear and rational modes of thought with limited symbol and picture making. Some examples of using metaphorical communication for processing the experience include:

1. "What are the walls that you face back at work or home, and how can you get over them?"

2. "What mountains in your life are you still climbing?"

3. "When do you need to re-orient your map at home?"

4. "When in your life do you need to get out of your boat and scout the rapids?"

5. "Who are your spotters or belayers back home?"

Each of these examples creates a picture for individuals from the real, felt, and lived experiences of the course and asking them to make connections and meanings with other aspects of their life. The experience then becomes a metaphor for them. Siegelman (1990) writes, "What gives metaphor its usefulness is the possibility of bridging or generalizing so that thought can cover a larger domain than originally. But what gives metaphor its vividness and resonance is its connection with the world of sensed and felt experience" (p. 7).

Below are some words that can be used to facilitate the use of metaphorical language. Carefully select your words to enable students to make pictures when they hear your words. This can help arouse their affect and connect unconscious processes.

1. poison	10. burned	19. exploded
2. imprisoned	11. wounded	20. whipped
3. strangled	12. betrayed	21. struggle
4. burst	13. starving	22. speeding
5. liberated	14. thirsty	23. violated
6. isolated	15. overflowing	24. abused
7. stranded	16. submerged	25. reborn
8. suffocated	17. trapped	26. smothered
9. drowning	18. set free	27. slapped

An example that contrasts the use of metaphorical language versus not using it would be the following. "It seems like the trapeze leap was a good experience for you" versus "Climbing up the ladder you seemed terrified and trapped and once you jumped you seemed unshackled and set free." You could then follow up these statements with "What were the chains that were keeping you stuck?" This type of question can provide stimuli for a rich debrief.

Metaphor Themes

There are some basic themes that metaphors communicate, which are common to all humans. These themes can be used as a resource, because people have already experienced them and need only to apply this universal knowledge to their particular situation. We are then using their understanding of these themes and bridging it with their current experience. This process is an example of the utilization approach. We are taking something that is already there and finding a way to use it as a metaphor. Below are some basic themes which are in no way exclusive. They are presented as stimuli to further promote your creativity and personal style in using metaphors and telling stories.

A. *Journey Theme*—This can be used when individuals or a group are beginning a new project, endeavor, task, career, or life course.

1. *Types of Journeys:*

    (a) Train
    (b) Automobile
    (c) Ship or Boat
    (d) Plane
    (e) Bicycle
    (f) On foot

2. *Trip Planning and Beginning:*

    (a) Planning and gathering information–research
    (b) Gathering supplies
    (c) Conditioning for the journey
    (d) Setting a goal
    (e) Orienting the map
    (f) Breaking inertia to get started
    (g) Taking the first step
    (h) Setting the sails

3. *Navigation:*

    (a) *Taking charge or responsibility*—who is the skipper, who is behind the wheel, helmsman, driver, pilot or conductor?
    (b) *Skills and attitude*— concentration, patience, paying attention, effort, focus, and ability to self-correct or re-orient.
    (c) *Direction*—staying on track, one foot after another, getting lost, wrong path, off the track, going in circles, put it in reverse, turning around, asking for and receiving directions or feedback, self-correction, and staying on course.
    (d) *Refueling*—resting, recharging, eddying out, making stops, missing the stop because too focused on time and destination, care of or lack of care for vehicle, maintenance issues versus task issues, and making the most of layovers.
    (e) *Dealing with obstacles*—how do you or your group deal with obstacles or crises? What kind of ride is it? Bumpy road, storms at sea, rapids, getting derailed, air pockets, debris on the track, blizzards, white out, fogged in, blacked out, out of gas, broken down, dead battery, and grounded.

4. *Destination*—pulling into port or station. Who is there to meet you? What is there? What are the rewards? What are the feelings—relief, exhilaration, accomplishment, or anxiety to head out again?

    Example: ''The group appeared to get derailed when Steve and Barry started arguing; no one emerged to be the conductor and get you back on track. What do you think is needed here to get this train going and arrive safely at our destination?''

B. *Healing Theme*—This can be used when there has been a setback, hurt, or an emotional wound exists. It is a valuable metaphor to use for interpersonal relations with couples, groups, and families.

    1. *Healing* is a process that takes time and effort. Paying attention to the wound and particular stages of healing will expedite the process.

2. *Grief model* for any kind of loss. From Elizabeth Kubler-Ross, we know the stages of grief: (a) Denial, (b) Anger, (c) Bargaining, (d) Depression, and (e) Acceptance.

3. *Medical Model*—this is taken from the medical pathology of tissues, or standard first aid. When there has been a deep cut or wound, the following stages of healing occur:

   (a) The pain, hurt, and bleeding of the hurt.
   (b) There is the bridge of new skin to cover the wound, the scab. It is extremely sensitive and can easily fall off, open the wound and start bleeding again. In human relations, one party may cause the other's scab to come off and open the hurt again. People need to be sensitive with each other when there has been a wound. The scab is the bridging of one party to patch it up, but this bridge needs to be attended to by both parties. Understanding and commitment by both parties to heal the wound is necessary.
   (c) The initial scab is knocked off and cleaned out, so the new skin can heal better. This is the airing of resentments and hurts to be able to start fresh without any dirt in the wound. It may be painful for the parties involved but will heal better than in the initial clotting stage. It is the resolution versus the covering over of the wound.
   (d) The new skin emerges being fresh, revitalized, and clean.
   (e) There always will be a trace of a scar; you won't forget it, but you can forgive the people involved.
   Example: "There appears to be a deep hurt or wound between the two of you, and you have continued to knock each other's delicate scab and opened the hurt and bleeding again. Would you like some support in cleaning out this wound, so you can both heal better, get some new skin, and get beyond this hurt?" Later, you can just use the word "scab" to evoke this healing process.

C. *Systems Theme*—This can be used with groups or families. The central point is that everyone is a member of a team or family and needs to work together.

   1. If one player, family member, or part of a machine is down, it affects all other parts and the total efficiency of the system.
   2. As in a factory, there are inputs, outputs, human resources, materials, and procedures, all of which are necessary and dependent on the other parts for success.
   3. The care of the machine is vital. Changing the oil, lubing, and greasing, making sure the engine runs properly, keeping the tires inflated, gas in the tank, not racing the engine, and making sure all parts of the machine are being attended to. This will make a smooth and efficient team, or group. Sports analogies can be used. Casey Stengel said, "It's easy getting the players. Getting them to play together is the hard part."
   Example: Bob worked as an auto mechanic manager and felt very stressed out at work. The instructor used the systems theme with him. "Bob, what happens when you run your autos without oil or changing the plugs, and how efficient can you be when you are constantly racing and never take time to grease your parts?"

D. *Cyclic and Natural Phenomena Themes*—this can be used with groups to point out the processes of nature and to expect the unexpected.

1. *Time* is a constant changer. What is new today is old tomorrow. Time never stops, and the world is in constant motion.
2. *Seasons,* flowers, and crops follow an endless consistent cycle. Birth, life, production, fruitfulness, old age, death, and rebirth again. Death of one animal is life to another.
3. *Natural calamities*—survival of the fittest. Storms, fires, avalanches, lightening storms, tornadoes, and death. We all experience crises and losses. It's the process of getting through these struggles safely that forces us to grow. New growth is the result of a fire. Starting over again is the continual rebirth.
   Example: "The best way to get through the storms of your life is to be ready and prepared for it. What do you need in your personal first aid kit to get through the storms to reach the calm after it?"

The process of becoming aware of the value of communicating metaphorically and developing your metaphor style and skills starts by asking yourself questions similar to the following:

1. "What does this situation remind me of?"

2. "How is this like something else?"

3. "How did I learn this?"

4. "What most clearly and completely symbolizes this experience?"

5. "How have other people or groups resolved this problem?"

6. "What could this situation or problem mean in terms of the development of the group?"

7. "How can the problem be a symbol for the entire group?"

8. "If the feelings among the group were a picture or image, what would it be?"

9. "Is there anything from the metaphor themes I can apply here?"

10. "How do I know this idea or suggestion is valid? What is the evidence that makes it convincing?"

11. "How can I reframe the problem into a resource or strength?"

12. "Is there an experience I can design for the students that would symbolize and be instrumental in developing a needed resource?"

It's then important to listen to yourself and to trust what comes up. There may be a story, experience, symbol, or ceremony. Many times it's just asking some new and different questions that engenders some new thoughts. Some of the ideas may seem crazy and illogical, but remember working with metaphors is not a linear and rational process. Much of its power comes from being indirect and talking to the unconscious. Many of a leader's most creative and effective ideas have remained as only a thought and censored from actually saying or doing it. So, it is important for you to take some risks and manage your own discomfort at the edge to create breakthroughs for your students and yourself.

Creating Metaphors for Experiences and Feelings

This section will explore how metaphors can be created from students' experiences and feelings. The purpose is to: (a) Give students a symbol, image, or story that can easily encapsulate their present experience and be easily retrieved at a later time; (b) Help students be aware of the metaphors they are making unconsciously which may prevent them from breaking through new edges; and (c) Improve students' capability to change their metaphors so as to foster more breakthroughs.

Metaphor Training

In developing metaphors for and from the adventure-based experience, participants need to learn what a metaphor is and the reasons for creating them. We encourage you to have a discussion early in the course, focusing on the value of making metaphors. Below are some of the points that you may want to cover. These have been touched on earlier in the text.

1. A metaphor is an image, symbol, story, or ceremony that stands for something else. It is the bridge or connection between two things. So, metaphors can help connect the adventure-based experience back to the home, school or office.

2. Metaphors can enhance the transfer of the experience; this is because memory is a series of images or pictures. If one's pictures are clear, graphic, and engaging, they will be easier to remember and use back home.

3. People think in images and metaphors unconsciously, and sometimes these images may prevent them from achieving personal growth. Being aware of one's metaphors can help in replacing old or outdated images with more useful ones.

4. At various times during the course, discussions will be held to explore and to create metaphors for what is transpiring.

Once students understand the importance of metaphor making, you can begin metaphor training. Below are some exercises that you may want to do with your groups in the first few days. The exercises will help create an understanding of the value of making metaphors and train the associative mind to make connections in this way. Only a few are presented here; for more suggestions, see Combs and Freedman (1990).

1. Pick two things or objects and have the group brainstorm how they are alike or similar. Start with some easy ones, then have students pick two things, and let the creative mind stretch in finding similarities.
   Examples: Tree and blade of grass: Each are alive, growing, longer than wide, stand erect, point to the sun, move with the wind, can be a source of nutrients to animals, can serve as protection for animals, and at times are cut down. Stove and Car: Each are a type of machine, use fuel to operate, have moving parts, take something from one point to another (stove: liquid to steam) and get hot while in use.

2. Have students pick an object from the outdoors and bring it to the group. Then have them create a simile about it. "This _____ is like a _____ ." Then take it the next step by saying "This _____ is like a _____ in that _____." You can have each person do it for their object, and when the group gets efficient, have the whole group do it for one person's object.

Examples: "This stick is like a building." ". . . in that it is straight and erect." "This pebble is like a marble in that it rolls away easily." "This feather is like a backscratcher in that I can reach hard to get areas."

3. Students can do the above exercise once it is mastered using the emotions as the simile stem.

Examples: "Sadness is like a stormy day in that it's gray and full of moisture." "Happiness is like a bird in that it can take you many places." "Anger is like a volcano in that when you explode, people get hurt."

4. Pick certain outcomes from an activity, like cooperation, trust, compassion, understanding, and exhilaration. Pick one word first and ask students, "If this was a picture or image, what would it be a picture or image of?"

Examples: "Cooperation could be a picture of one hand helping another." "Exhilaration could be an image of an air balloon floating upwards." Hopefully, from this start, you can create your own metaphor training exercises that are specific to your setting.

Metaphor and Affect

On an adventure-based course, we know that emotions are intensified; sometimes to the point that words can't describe what is going on. If a student is in this new territory, a metaphor can be discovered or created to bring the experience back into the circle of comfort, where the experience can be familiar and known. Here, the metaphor becomes a bridge from the unknown new territory back to the known and predictable.

Siegelman (1990) found that figurative language springs from strong feelings or affect that is unable to be conveyed in any other way. By staying with the metaphor and nurturing it along, the student's responses to it deepen. When we hear a student use a metaphor, especially in a time of strong affect, it becomes a way of making sense or connecting this experience with the rest of his or her life story. Be gentle and easy with the metaphor, allowing the student to ease it out and take its own form. Your role is that of a midwife helping the birthing process. Using the metaphor later with the student will help stimulate these deep feelings.

Metaphors and feelings are initially experienced in our bodies. This is because our first affective experiences as a child were housed in the body. Our "lump in throat", "the pounding heart", and "knot in the stomach" all describe feelings. We can facilitate the expression of feelings and metaphors if we can get students to focus on their bodies and describe that phenomena. In a way, learning to identify feelings from the bodily experience is an affective education, especially for some people who are unaware of their emotional domain. Sensitizing the person to their differing body experiences can help illuminate what they are feeling. One student, Mary, reported, "When I was younger and experiencing many physical symptoms, I went to a doctor. He told me they were all in my head and to forget about it. I thought then I was just a head case and crazy.'' When Mary felt things in the body, she then felt crazy. This kind of miseducation about the body and feelings is common. The doctor would have been more helpful if he said, ''Your symptoms are all in your body and that tells me that you're feeling a lot, and it's very natural. It may help to talk to someone about your feelings.'' As we mentioned earlier, the adventure-based course can become an excellent vehicle to learn about one's feelings. Creating metaphors from feelings will not only help on the course, but will be a valuable tool to bring home.

Making Experiences and Feelings Into Metaphors

Experiences and feelings can be made into metaphors when we can create an image, picture, or symbol. David Grove (1989) writes, ''You know when you have a metaphor when you can draw it'' (p. 7). The objective then is to ask the right questions and take the time to allow students' experiences and feelings to emerge into images. The flow chart for this process is below:

Experiences	Feelings
↓	↓
Images	Body
	↓
	Images

Some questions to help guide you when making metaphors for students are found below. Try to catch students when their experiences and feelings are heightened. This will usually be in the S-1 experience, the moments before the success or retreat, or as they move into the success and S+1 experience, the moments after the success.

Metaphor-Making Questions

Some of these questions are drawn from the work of Grove (1989).

1. ''What are you feeling now?''

2. ''When you're feeling _____, where do you feel it in your body?''

3. ''Where about in your _____ do you feel _____?'' (Get specific location.)

4. ''Is it on the inside or the outside?''

5. ''When you're feeling _____ and it's in your _____, does it have a size or shape?''

6. ''When you're feeling _____ and it's in your _____, what is it like?''

7. ''What kind of _____ could it be?''

103

8. "If you had to draw a picture of your _____ (feeling) when it's in your _____ (body part), what would it be?"

9. "Is there anything else about _____ (images created)?"

10. Talking to the metaphor: "What would _____ like to have happen?"

11. To the metaphor: "What would _____ like to do?"

12. To the metaphor: "And as _____ (metaphor) moves, what happens next?"

13. To the person as a way of redirecting to the metaphor: "What would you like to have happen with _____ (metaphor)"; "When you want to _____ _____ (get rid of metaphor), what does _____ (the metaphor) want to do?"

14. "If this experience was an image or picture, what would it be?"

15. "If you had to draw a picture of this experience, what would you draw?"

16. "When you are experiencing _____, what are you feeling?"

17. "When you are experiencing _____ and feeling _____ _____, where are you experiencing _____?" (Follow feelings into metaphor questions.)

18. "Is there anything else about _____ (experience into an image)?"

In establishing a metaphor and then talking to the metaphor, you help create and define the metaphor. It then has its own identity with certain intentions and qualities that can give the students more information about themselves. Many times a metaphor in the body has been an ineffective way to solve a problem. Talking to the metaphor and allowing it to change, you facilitate a change in feelings and more constructive use of the metaphor.

Some examples of how this is used will help clarify the process. Brian, who was 28 years old, felt very nervous and anxious at the start of a corporate teambuilding day. When he located this feeling in his body, it was in his heart, which was "moving fast." When we asked, "Moving fast like what?", he responded like a "sleek locomotive." The sleek locomotive wanted to move and get going; it had a schedule. We asked the sleek locomotive if it could "stand waiting at a station to get fuel and directions on where it's going"? He laughed and realized how his locomotive wanted to move but wasn't sure where it was headed. Throughout the day, we returned to his locomotive metaphor and asked questions, like, "How could it slow down when it's necessary?"; "Are there stops that would be important to make in life versus racing to the destination"; "Who is the conductor of this locomotive?"; "Can you slow down for this next activity and possibly let some others get on with you?"; and "When you are at the office, when does your locomotive get away from you?"

Obviously, Brian's locomotive didn't just emerge for the corporate teambuilding day. He was able to see that it was with him at many moments in his work day. Also, he was able to externalize it and look at it, rather than it driving him, unconsciously. He had fun playing with the metaphor and experimented with slowing it down during the day. This helped change some of his feelings associated with it and let him feel empowered by being in charge of the locomotive's schedule.

Maxine was a 32-year-old woman on a course for individuals in recovery from drugs and alcohol. Whenever a new activity commenced, she felt anxious about her performance. When she located this feeling in her body, it was in her chest and it felt heavy. In response to "heavy like what?", she said like a "rock." When asked, "What kind of rock could this heavy rock be?", she said like a "heavy brick." We then asked the metaphor, "What would it like to do?" She said, "Go out and let her breathe." We asked, "Can the heavy brick move out?", and she responded, "No." "What could help the heavy brick move off your chest?", we then asked. She responded, "If I take a deep breath and exhale hard, I can move it off." Once outside of her, the brick became a "shiny shield" to help fend off others' demands of her. We eventually helped her transform her "shiny shield" into a "talking shield" that could assertively tell others to give her space and let her feel more protected. Later, during a private discussion with her, she discovered that the "heavy brick" had been there since a time of sexual abuse with her uncle at an early age. It had served as a protection for her for all those years. Now she knew how to expel the "brick" and use a "talking shield" to take care of herself. As we mentioned, many of these metaphors were created as a means to solve some kind of problem, and then the metaphor itself became a symptom of the problem. During the course, Maxine was encouraged to breathe deeply and expel her brick and tell the group from the "talking shield" what she needed. When she did this, she breathed better, felt empowered, and went ahead and took risks.

Using metaphors can help make important affective shifts for students, even without knowing the content or the purpose of the metaphor. In working with Maxine, we didn't need to know about the abuse, as she was making shifts initially without knowing this content. In many cases, it is safer to work within the metaphor than to expose a possible trauma. Similarly, it is best to try to help students find additional resources rather than exhume problems, unless that is the focus of the course and within the scope of your skills and training.

In summary, you can help create metaphors from the experiences and feelings of students which will assist them in remembering the experience and also help promote transfer and generalization. We suggest that you use the information presented in this section as a jumping off point for metaphor making, and that you go ahead, get wet, and have fun in the water.

Reluctant Individuals

From time to time you will work with individuals who are reluctant to share their thoughts and feelings with other group members. As a result, you will want to draw them out in an effort to have them contribute to the group experience. The reasons to get these individuals involved is that the verbal give and take and sharing of ideas is an essential part of the group experience. Hearing different ideas and perspectives is one of the goals of processing. In addition, it is likely that members who have a difficult time sharing in this group also have trouble talking in front of others in their home environment. By getting these individuals to participate, they may develop a sense of confidence about speaking up. Concomitantly, other group members will benefit from hearing the thoughts and feelings of the reserved member. Another reason to try and draw out participants is to help them explore things in greater depth. They may present information on a surface level. Through questioning you can assist them in being more introspective and possibly help them gain more from the experience.

Occasionally, group members want to speak but do not because they are afraid of what other members might think of them. They envision people laughing at them or thinking that they are stupid. It is important to try and involve these members so that they can come to realize that they are focusing on the worst possible scenario which is not likely to occur at all. Other reasons that people might be reluctant to get involved are that they are not committed to the group, they do not trust the leader or some of the other group members, or that the leader or another member of the group dominates discussions, which causes others to sit back and listen rather than contribute.

Frequently, you can tell when members want to speak and can often elicit their comments by simply nodding your head or gesturing in their direction. Additional statements that have been adapted from Jacobs, Harvill and Masson (1988) are "Go ahead," "It looks as though you are thinking. Would you like to share your thoughts?" "You seem to be reacting to something. Is there something that you would like to share?" "It seems that you were relating to his statement. What are your thoughts?" "Julie, you have been rather quiet today. Is there something on your mind?"

The challenge to drawing out members of the group is to get them to speak and share their thoughts and feelings. At the same time they will need to have the option to decline and not be put on the spot. One technique is to look at a member who is being quiet for a brief moment, and with your eyes invite the person to speak. If the person does not choose to talk, then you can shift your eyes away which will then give the person the right to pass.

You can invite the person to speak by using a tentative voice and trying not to focus the attention of the group on that person. For example, you may say "Bert, I notice that you have been quiet throughout out discussion. We would like to hear from you if you want to comment." At this point you would want to scan the group with your eyes rather than staring at Bert. If he doesn't comment in a reasonable amount of time, you can open things back up and say something such as, "Who would like to share what they are thinking about?"

According to Jacobs, Harvill and Masson (1988) there are two primary ways to draw reluctant students out. They are called the direct method and the indirect method. A brief explanation of both methods and some specific examples follow:

Direct Method

The direct method refers to the procedure of simply asking individuals if they want to comment or react to what is going on. Some specific examples of direct questions that you could use are: (A) "Kent, you seemed to be having lots of fun on the wild walk this morning. Would you like to share your impression of the activity?", (b) "Barbara, we have heard a lot of different perspectives on how the wall went. Is there anything that you would like to add?", (c) "Richard, you have been very quiet since we got back from the peak ascent. Is there something on your mind?"

As suggested above, using eye contact is a valuable technique for eliciting comments from group members. This is especially true when people are waiting to talk. By acknowledging people with your eyes and a light head nod you can often let them know that you are looking forward to their comment. This technique can be used in a more direct fashion should you like. When speaking to the entire group, you can maintain eye contact with a specific member; this acknowledges that you would like that person to speak, but also gives him or her an out should they not want to comment. For example, while looking mainly at Molly, you say, "Does anyone else want to say something about climbing?" You can then scan the group and return your eyes to Molly. If she is not ready to respond, then you can shift your eyes to other members of the group.

Indirect Method

There are three indirect methods that you can use to involve reluctant members. They are the use of dyads, rounds and written exercises. The value of using these techniques have been explained earlier. When the dyads come back together you may want to use some of the following types of questions to invite students to talk: (a) "Who would like to share what you were talking about?", (b) "What were some of your thoughts about solo?", (c) "What kinds of things came to mind when you talked about how you resolve conflicts with your partner?", (d) "Does anyone want to comment on what you discussed in your pairs?", and (e) "Mike, would you mind sharing with us some of the things that you talked about in your dyad?"

This procedure is usually effective because individuals have something to say as a result of the discussion that they have just completed. Another way to structure this activity is for you to be a member of a dyad with the reluctant individual. During your discussion, you can either seek to find out why the person chooses to be silent and/or give the person encouragement for his/her ideas and suggestions that you would like him/her to share that information with the larger group.

Rounds are another valuable technique for getting reluctant members to contribute. If while doing a round the reluctant individual appears to be hesitant or anxious, you can skip that person by saying something like "we'll give you a little more time to think" and then come back to him/her after everyone else has contributed. Also, you can make it easier on that person by starting the round with the person sitting next to him or her and ending up on the reluctant individual. This also makes it possible for you to ask for more information from that person since he/she was the last to comment when the round is ended. An example of a round that you could use is: "In a word or a phrase, what was the most difficult part of the acid river for you? Think about that for a moment, then I'm going to ask everyone to share their thoughts."

Written exercises can be used to help reluctant individuals contribute. This activity tends to be indirect and nonthreatening because your are only asking members what they wrote. You can structure the activity around a journal entry, compiling a list or giving the group a series of sentences to complete. After individuals have completed their writing, you can ask them to share their responses. With their ideas written down in front of them, individuals are less likely to mind since they are now simply being asked to share their written responses. An example of a written exercise that you might want to consider is to say something like: "In your journals I would like for you to respond to the following incomplete sentences: (a) My high point of the day was _____, (b) Something that I did today that I feel proud of is _____, (c) Something that I would like to work on tomorrow is _____, and (d) One way that the group can help me is _____."

Redirecting

On occasion, you may work with a student that you would like to stop talking. For the purpose of this section we will use the term of redirecting to indicate that you are trying to intercept the flow of communication in a nonpunitive manner to help the group move in a specific direction. Some possible reasons that you would want to intervene are when an individual is (a) rambling, (b) arguing, or (c) dominating the session. Other reasons that you may consider redirecting the flow of conversation are if you want to shift the focus of the discussion or if you are running out of time.

Timing is one of the most important and difficult factors to consider when trying to redirect an individual or groups' energy. Whenever possible, you want to intervene quickly, before someone rambles too long or argues for an extended block of time. At the same time, you want to be careful not to cut off a worthwhile statement. Personal experience and an awareness of the patterns of the speaker and the responses of the group in general will help guide you in making the right decision.

Similarly, your tone of voice and inflection while redirecting will have an impact on how what you say comes across to the person and group. If it is viewed as critical or angry it is likely to have a negative impact even if the words that you use are carefully chosen. Calming yourself, and trying to understand the motives of the speaker are helpful steps prior to intervening.

A positive practice to use when redirecting is to explain to the individual and group why you are stopping what is happening. By taking the time to discuss your motives you are preventing members from having to try to invent their own. Without providing a rationale they are likely to wonder such things as, "Why doesn't the leader like me"? or "How come my opinion doesn't matter"? For example, if the discussion has begun to get a little heated and you are concerned about the direction it is going you may want to say something like, "Dave, let me break in here if you don't mind. I want to remind you of some of the ground rules that we set. That is, that we listen to each other and accept that everyone is different and that we try to accept that everyone has a right to their own ideas and ways of doing things." Or if you are concerned about time you could interject something along the lines of "Marion, I wonder if it would be possible for you to sum up your discussion in the next moment or two. We're running short of time and energy and need to move on."

Two nonverbal techniques that you can use are to avoid eye contact while the person is talking or to give a slight hand signal, similar to a traffic cop which you hope will let the speaker know that you would like him or her to wrap it up. If these types of subtle hints do not work, then you will need to use a more direct verbal approach. The following are a list of potential statements that you could use to get the flow of conversation away from one specific person and back to the other group members:

Kent, let me cut in and stop you in order to give others an opportunity to speak. What reactions did some other people have to the ropes course?

Marilyn, let me stop you here to say a couple of things. First . . .

How about others? What were some of your perceptions of how the day went?

Mike, I would like to hold off on your comments until we have heard from a few other folks first.

Ann, I notice that you are always ready to speak first. I'm wondering if there is any specific reason behind that?

Let me stop you, because I don't think that you are listening to each other.

Steve, you have some valid points and I want to give others an opportunity to speak also.

Hunter, I'm aware that you're first to speak often. I wonder if you'd be willing to experiment with going last and see how that feels.

Beth, I notice that you are always ready to speak first. I'm wondering if you would like some feedback from the group about how they feel about this pattern?

I would like you to stop, since it doesn't seem like you are getting anywhere.

Additional Processing Questions

In addition to using the levels of processing questions, there are times that you will want to ask questions that focus on specific thoughts, feelings, and behaviors. The following questions, some of which have been adapted from Knapp (1984), are useful to refer to when preparing for discussions.

Trust and Support

1. What did it feel like to have your physical safety entrusted to the group?

2. What are the similarities and differences in the way you supported each other here and the way you support others back at home, school or the office?

3. What impact does trust have in your relationship with others at home, school or at work?

4. What is the relationship between managing risk and establishing a support system?

Communication

1. What were some of the effective forms of communication that you used in completing this task? Ineffective forms of communication?

2. How were differences in opinion handled?

3. In what ways could the group's process of communication be improved to enhance its problem-solving skills?

4. How could you improve your communication and networking?

Making Group Decisions

1. How did the group make decisions for completing the tasks during the day?

2. Were you satisfied with the manner in which the group made decisions?

3. Were decisions made by one or several individuals?

4. Did everyone express his or her opinion when a choice was available?

5. What did you like about the manner in which the group made decisions? What didn't you like?

6. What is the best way for this group to make decisions?

Cooperating

1. What are some specific examples of when the group cooperated during the activity/day?

2. How did it feel to cooperate?

3. How did cooperative behavior lead to the successful completion of the tasks presented during the day?

4. What are the rewards of cooperating?

5. What can you personally do to produce a cooperative environment at home or work?

Teamwork

1. How well do you think you did?

2. How effective were you in completing the task?

3. How efficient were you?

4. How did you develop your plan of action?

5. What is the relationship between input into the plan and commitment to action?

6. What were the differences between having a common vision versus not having a vision?

Problem-Solving

1. Have you noticed any patterns in the way you solve problems? Are they productive? Unproductive?

2. What effect did planning time have on the process?

3. How well did you execute your plan?

4. On a scale of 1–10, how committed were you to executing the plan?

5. What are the similarities and differences between the ways in which you have approached solving problems here and the way that you approach them at home, school, or work?

6. What would need to change at in order to enhance your problem-solving ability?

Leadership Roles

1. Who assumed leadership roles during the activity/day?

2. What were the behaviors that you would describe as demonstrating leadership?

3. How did the group respond to these leadership behaviors?

4. When and how did the leadership role change during the activity/day?

5. Was it difficult to assume a leadership role in this group? Why?

6. What are the characteristics and qualities of a good leader?

7. What specific skills do you need to develop to become a more effective leader?

Following Others

1. Do you consider yourself a good follower? Was this an important role during the activity/day?

2. What type of leader was it easiest to follow?

3. Did the manner in which the feedback was given make a difference to you? Explain.

4. What was difficult about being a follower?

Self-Statements

1. Did you criticize yourself or put yourself down during the activity/day?

2. What did you say to yourself?

3. Do you usually get upset with yourself when you make a mistake or do not achieve perfection?

4. What could you say to yourself to counteract the put-down message?

5. What are some ways in which you were successful during the activity/day?

6. What self-messages did you give yourself when you were successful?

7. How can you increase your positive self-messages in the future?

Giving and Receiving Feedback

1. What are some examples of when you received feedback during the activity/day? How did it feel?

2. Did the manner in which the feedback was given make a difference to you?

3. What are some examples of when you gave feedback during the day?

4. How did you express appreciation for another during the day?

5. What are some appreciations that you did not express?

6. Do you typically express appreciations?

7. How can you improve your skills in giving and receiving feedback?

Respecting Personal Differences

1. What are some of the significant differences among group members?

2. How did these differences strengthen the group-as-a-whole during the day?

3. What would this group be like if there were very few differences among the group members?

4. What specific instances did being different help or hinder the group from reaching its objectives?

5. How can you increase your ability to respect and utilize personal differences?

Closure Questions

1. What did you learn about yourself?

2. What did you learn about other group members?

3. What did you do today that you are particularly proud of?

4. How can you use what you learned today in other situations?

5. What beliefs about yourself and the other group members were reinforced during the day?

6. What specific skill are you going to improve as a result of this course?

Goal Setting and Personal Action Plans

This section of the text can be used for two purposes. We are presenting this as an activity for helping course participants develop personal goals for themselves that they can strive for after they complete the course. However, it also can be used to help you establish personal goals that you would like to accomplish in order to become a better facilitator. Using some of the information that you have gained from this text and feedback that you have received from people that you work with, you can develop a plan for increasing your skills.

When working with course participants, begin by asking them to identify behaviors, thoughts, or emotional patterns that they have become aware of during the course. Discuss alternatives to those patterns, identify sources of support and ways to reward themselves for meeting their goals. Course participants can do this activity on their own, in discussion with you, or this can be undertaken as a group activity; using the brainstorming abilities of all the members to help generate potential action plans for each individual.

The activity sheet found in table 3 has been adapted from Gerstein (1988). It can be used to assist individuals in identifying aspects of those patterns that they would like to change or modify and help them develop a strategy for making those changes. When developing goals and action plans, the following points should be kept in mind. Goals should be:

1. Desirable—based on something that individuals truly want.

2. Achievable—able to stretch a person, but not beyond the bounds of what is reasonable given an individual's strengths and limitations.

3. Concrete and Specific—includes what, when, how, where, and who.

4. Measurable—able to be evaluated in some quantitative and/or qualitative way.

5. Broken Down Into Small Steps—stated in a manner that allows individuals to take one small step at a time.

6. Immediate—can be initiated in the very near future.

7. Written—an unrecorded goal is only a wish.

Table 3. Personal Action Plan Worksheet

A. *What Are You Doing Now?*—Describe what you are doing that you would like to change?

B. *What Do You Want To Do?*—Describe what you want. Explain how you would like to change the situation.

C. *Goal Development*—Develop one or two goals based on the changes that you would like to make.

   1.

   2.

D. *Make A Plan*

   1.   What is the first step to take in order to reach your goal(s)?

   2.   What additional steps do you need to take to reach your goal(s)?

   3.   What obstacles could prevent you from reaching your goal(s)?

   4.   How will you overcome these obstacles or roadblocks?

   5.   What types of support will help you reach your goal(s)?

   6.   When and how will you implement your plan?

E. *Make A Commitment*

   1.   What positive outcomes may occur if you attain your goal(s)?

   2.   What negative outcomes may occur if you attain your goal(s)?

F. *Succeeding*

   1.   How will you know when you have attained your goal(s)?

   2.   What reward will you provide for yourself when your goal(s) has been attained?

Processing Activities

As adventure-based instructors, we are always searching for activities that can be used with the diverse groups we instruct and varied settings that we find ourselves working in. This section of the text provides a variety of exercises for you to experiment with. They are presented in a sequential manner that compliments the information discussed in the levels of processing section. Specifically, this section is broken-up into exercises for trust, awareness, responsibility, and experimentation and transfer. It ends with a few comments that we've labeled "Keynotes and Cautions" that are presented as reminders of how these activities are best used.

Trust Building

What follows are processing activities that you can use to build trust and bring students from awareness through responsibility to experimentation and transfer of learning. The exercises can be used as stimuli for your processing groups and as the thread that binds and weaves together diverse adventure activities with participants' emotional experiences.

Trust is an essential and vital component of adventure-based programs. During a course, students need to trust themselves during activities such as the ropes course, kayaking, solo, rock climbing, and marathon. They also need to trust other individuals, to administer first aid and provide for an evacuation resulting from a serious injury in the field, if necessary, and to work out group problems.

The development of a group follows a sequence that consists of trust, data flow, goals, and social control. Each stage is dependent on the stage prior to it. Without trust, people won't speak freely of their concerns or personal life (data flow). If data flow hasn't developed adequately, it will be very difficult to set group goals and make group decisions. Social control or procedures of a group is the final stage. It is contingent on the ability of the group to establish goals. Therefore, trust is the foundation of makeup of a successful group. The purpose and objectives of trust building are to allow students to (a) speak freely and honestly about their feelings, (b) take new risks, such as rock climbing, changing behavior, solo, etc., and (c) feel comfortable enough with the group to feel the sharing, warmth, and power of being a cohesive entity.

Trust building is most effective when done early in the course, the first few days and then gradually continued throughout the course. Some trust building exercises that you may want to experiment with follow:

1. *Adjective Game*—To learn everyone's name, one student starts by saying an adjective for how he or she feels now and his or her name. The next student repeats the first student's name and adjective and then his/her own. The third student repeats the first and second students' name and adjective and then his/her own. This proc-

ess continues around the entire circle. Other ways that this activity can be used are to pick a fruit, vegetable, or animal that you most identify with and your name; or, pick something you're good at and then your name. "I am a singer, Tom."

2. *Introducing Each Other*—This is an excellent first night activity. In dyads, one student talks about himself/herself, i.e., interests, his/her family, why he/she is on the course, and dreams. The other student just listens for four or five minutes. Switch the roles, then back in the group have students introduce their partner to the crew. In addition, when students introduce each other, they can state what aspect of their partner they were most impressed with. Finally, everyone can discuss how it felt having someone talk about them. This is also a good way to focus on using appropriate listening skills.

3. *Talk About Trust*—First in animals. How do you know an animal trusts you? What behavior does it exhibit? How does an animal know you trust it? How do you know when people trust you? What are the behavioral cues? How do you know when you trust someone? What behavioral cues exist?

4. *Trust Statements*—In dyads have students complete this sentence, while the other person just listens. "In order for me to trust you, you should _____, i.e., look at me when I speak, help me on the trail." Have each student do this for four or five minutes. Encourage students not to engage in conversation. Let them struggle with continually completing the sentence. "What things came out?" "What commonalities do you share?" "How did it feel struggling for answers?"

5. *Appreciations*—There are several different types of appreciations. Here are a few that we have used with great success. (a) Students can share something positive about the person to their right or left, and then continue to go around that way. This is a good way to end a group session around the fire; (b) Select a student who had a hard day, either from the activities or from the other students. Each student shares an appreciation with this one student. He/she should be encouraged not to sabotage compliments and just listen and accept them. On a long course try to bombard each student at least once.

6. *Trust fall*—Have the whole brigade do a trust fall from a stump or rock. One student falls backward into the arms of the others.

7. *Trust Walk*—(a) In dyads, one student is blindfolded and the other leads him/her through a variety of experiences; (b) Form a line and have all the students blindfolded. One person is not blindfolded and is the only one who can speak. Students hold on to whatever they can and follow each other nonverbally.

8. *Feeling Word*—To help students become more aware of their feelings, and also to get a feel for where your group is at. Have each person say the first feeling that is with them right at the moment. This is good if it's done fast. You can utilize this to start group sessions, and also end them.

9. *Blind Line*—Have students either put sleeping bags over their heads and body or a bandanna on their eyes. Give each student a number (1–10 or 1–12) secretly and have them line up in order non-verbally. Whatever way they can do it without talking. Questions to ask include: "How did you feel?" "Were you frustrated?"

10. *Nourishing Game*—Have each student share with the group someone that has made them feel good today and how it was done.

Figure 23. Trust Fall

11. *Good Trait*—Have everyone in group share a good trait they have. Another alternative is to share their greatest success of the day.

12. *Interviews*—Break up into groups of three or four. Each group selects one person to be interviewed. Other members of the group can ask him or her any questions they want. The person being interviewed has the option to pass on any question. Change roles until every member of the group has been interviewed. Ask "What kind of questions are easiest for you to answer?" "Hardest?"

13. *Concentric Circle Unfolding*—Count off by 2's. Form two circles facing each other, one inside the other. Discuss topics with one person listening, the other talking, then switch. Practice non-judgemental listening. Groups move opposite ways, so each topic gets different people together. Topics can be anything that you want. Here are some suggestions:

   1. Most memorable experience in the last two weeks.

2. Someplace in world I'd like to go.

3. Hero or heroine of childhood.

4. Person I want most to impress.

5. What skill would I like to master.

Follow this up with a discussion. Some questions that you may want to include are: ''Who was easiest to talk to?'' ''Hardest?'' ''What made them so?'' ''Any difference talking first or second?'' ''What topic was hardest?'' ''Which sex was easier to talk to?''

14. *Sentence Completions*—To help process any experience, have students complete some of the following sentences.

A. I learned today

B. I was afraid when

C. I liked

D. I disliked

E. I'm unhappy when

F. I'm cool when I

G. I feel good when

H. When I'm mad I

I. My favorite place is

J. Something I never told anyone is

K. What people like best in me

L. I'd like my parents to

M. I'm concerned about

N. Other people in this group

O. I usually avoid

P. What I hate most

Q. My friends are

R. When I'm frustrated I usually

S. What I fear the most

T. I am really

U. Most people don't know that I

Awareness

This part of the curriculum is designed for students to learn more about themselves via the adventure-based activities. It is an opportunity to collect data about one's thoughts, feelings, and actions. Students are provided with information regarding the

122

interdependence and integration of thoughts, feelings, and actions in the learning process. The intention is to achieve personal relevancy that can emerge from the activities and the course. This can happen when students learn from activities about themselves and others, as opposed to retaining fond memories about activities.

Repeated actions to the same thoughts and feelings are called patterns. Patterns are unconscious or conditioned roles or ways of being that we fall into during our interactions with superiors, the opposite sex, fear, alienation, groups, or whatever the situation may be. Some traditional patterns are: the know it all, the loser, the competitor, the dumb role, the passive one, the macho, the arguer, the intellectual, and the compromiser. Whatever patterns students possess usually surface more in an adventure setting than at home, because of the intensity of the experience. This makes patterns a vital educational tool. Going back to our model, the more a student learns about his or her patterns when in disequilibrium, the more conscious control and responsibility they'll have in making the transfer of learning personally relevant at home. The purposes and objectives of Awareness exercises are to: (a) allow students to become aware of and integrate their thoughts, feelings, and actions, (b) allow students to see patterns that arise; (c) explore the relevancy of patterns on a course and at home; (d) make unconscious roles and patterns conscious; and (e) allow students to see how patterns are serving them and what alternative actions are available.

These exercises should be started when you feel that there is a sufficient trust level in the group. Continue to work with the awareness exercises throughout the course.

1. Have a brief discussion as to what roles or patterns are. We all have them, and this course is an opportunity to look at some of them. Lay a gentle seed.

2. In group activities, such as the wall initiative, the beam, jogging, swimming, group decisions, and setting and breaking camp:

   A. Keep journals—ask students directly after an activity to jot down a few notes. "What were your feelings during the activity?" "What did you like and dislike?" "What were some of the statements that you were telling yourself during the activity?" "What were you doing?" "Were you uncomfortable doing anything? If so, what?" "Were any of your reactions typical of you? If so, what?" The first time just let them write, ask if any reactions. Next time talk about how a person's thoughts, feelings, actions work together and off of each other. Let them write down their thoughts, feelings and actions that they took. "How typical is this?" is an appropriate question to ask.

   B. Sometimes preface one of these activities with "Be aware of the role that you're taking here." "What part are you playing?"

   C. Other times at the end of an activity, ask the students to all share what role they thought they took. Ask them to think if this role is similar to what they do at home.

   D. Something to try once is to have each student play the opposite role and do the same activity.

   E. Discuss with students early in the course how rare an opportunity they have to experiment with different behaviors. Statements such as, "No one knows you," "Be whoever you want," "Try things differently on the course," help to set an open and free atmosphere. Do exercises when you feel it's a good time. Be in touch with yourself, and your students' levels of disequilibrium.

3. *Forced Choice*—Make two parallel lines in the dirt, or on a trail about eighteen feet apart. Ask students to decide on one choice or the other and stand behind the respective line. Ask them would you rather be:

ice cream or cake	chair or table
hammer or nail	spender or saver
pitcher or batter	forest or ocean
lover or loved one	helper or helpee

"What were your feelings?" "Which were hardest and easiest?" "What were the statements that you were telling yourself?" "Did you move quickly or hesitate?" "Did any patterns emerge in your choices?"

4. *Line Continuum*—Make two lines on the ground parallel to each other. One line is the highest point on a straight line and the other the lowest point. Students should line up in a straight line, one person per slot by rating themselves on this continuous line for the characteristics of:

leader-follower	optimist-pessimist
aggressive-passive	listener-talker
giver-taker	sensitive-cold

Select any combinations that are apropos, or make up your own. Once students are in a straight line rank ordered, ask if anyone disagrees with the order. If so, have them put people in the spot they feel they belong. Let any student who wants to change the order do so. This allows students to rate themselves and see how others perceive them.

Discussion questions can include: "How did you feel about the spot you put yourself at?" "What were your feelings in lining up?" "Were you uncomfortable or did you feel fine?" "How did you feel when someone moved you?" "Are there other times that you feel this way?" "What were some of your reasons for putting yourself where you did?" Keep things focused in a positive manner. Ask students if they see any specific patterns. You can use this exercise a number of times on the course as a benchmark to show growth or change.

5. *Ten Commandments—Discussion*

   A. "What were the rules of your house as you were growing up?" "What did you have to abide by?"

   B. "What were the 'shoulds' and 'shouldn'ts' of your peer group as you grew up?"

6. *Opposite Roles*—Have students pick partners and be aware of their pattern of choosing or waiting to be chosen. Each pair is to have a thumb wrestle, slap fight, and push fight. When they have finished, have each student identify his/her pattern in those activities; the competitor, playful, apathetic, serious, etc. Students are now to choose new partners and play the opposite role in the activities. Discuss how the new role felt, hard or uncomfortable, and what they liked about their original role. This exercise can be fun.

7. *Postures*—Ask students to pick partners and non-verbally have one acquire an inferior posture and the other a superior posture. Actually have them stand over or on top of each other. Have them switch, nonverbally being aware of how they feel making the transition. Discuss how students felt about being superior and inferior. "Which role was most comfortable?" "Which role do you usually acquire?" If you select a leader of the day, this can lead to a discussion of how you feel about being the leader and follower, and how would you like the leader to lead.

8. In a group discussion have students share a personal pattern that they have become aware of on the course. Then have students share how this pattern serves them. What is the benefit or "goodies"' they get by holding that pattern? Examples are, "I compromise myself all the time with people; what I get from it is that people like me, I'm easy to get along with, and I don't create waves." "I'm always a leader and tell people what to do. I get attention and it feels good." This exercise lets students become aware and take responsibility for their patterns. Do this activity towards the latter half of the course when the trust is built and students have a good feel for patterns. It is best if you go first and model the type of statement that you want people to make.

9. *Sculpturing*—In this exercise, students will position themselves as a multiperson sculpture or statue. They will have to decide who stands next to whom and in what posture or stance. For example, one person may be standing pointing a finger while another is kneeling below with his or her hands out, palms out. You can do the whole group or subgroups. When they are positioned, they are nonverbal and asked to be aware of their experience and feelings in that position.

   You may want to have a director who positions people and shapes them to have the appropriate expression and stance. You may want to pick a scene to depict like cooking dinner or doing map and compass. Processing questions can include: How do you feel in this position? What would you like to say anyone in the sculpture? What stops you from saying it? What postures and positions would you rather be in? How can you bring this about when you find yourself in the original position?

Responsibility

To some degree, many of us live in a cloud. This cloud limits our here and now awareness and personal responsibility. The disequilibrium that is created by participating in an adventure-based course provides an opportunity to wake up, reown, and make changes in our lives. The theory and techniques from Gestalt therapy can help us facilitate our students to take more responsibility on the course and in their life. Gestalt means wholeness. A Gestalt premise is that our cloud is made up of unfinished situations, resentments, dreams, and projections, which rise to emergence, at times seeking a form of expression. When we focus on these elements we're ignoring or blind to what we're currently experiencing, i.e., our environment while hiking, blisters on our feet, the beauty of nature, or how we are affecting others.

A goal of Gestalt is to return to wholeness by helping individuals to become aware of, responsible for, reclaim, and integrate their fragmented parts. Integration releases a surge of energy that was used to suppress these emotions. Students become more aware of themselves and the environment. This permits more responsibility for their feelings, thoughts, and actions. The following activities are valuable to use after the awareness phase of the course or when issues emerge. The objectives and purpose of the responsibility exercises are to allow the student to: (a) take responsibility for their thoughts, feelings, and actions; (b) be aware of their here and now experience physically, mentally, and emotionally, (c) discharge and deal constructively with their resentments; and, (d) take more control and responsibility for their lives. Ways in which you can facilitate for responsibility are:

125

1. Have your students speak in "I statements" as opposed to "you statements." This encourages students to own what they're saying. "When I get tired of hiking, all I want to do is sit down," as opposed to: "When you get tired of hiking, all you want to do is sit down."

2. Talk about responsibility and "Who controls you?" and "Who makes you do things?" One of the values of experiential education, is the immediacy of consequences. If students don't put their tarp up well and it rains, they get wet. Students need to become responsible for all their actions.

3. When you're at a rest stop while hiking or paddling, have your students complete this sentence. "I am aware of _____." Allow them to say it about five times, filling the blank with whatever they are aware of right then. Statements that they might make include: "I am aware of the wind"; "I am aware that John's boot is untied"; and "I am aware of a fly on my leg." This helps students cut through their own clouds. When possible this activity should be coupled with a solo walk afterwards, this promotes an increased awareness of the environment.

4. *Projection Exercise*—(a) Have your students bring back an item from the woods. In the circle, have them become that object and make I statements about it. Examples include: "I am a leaf"; "I am yellow"; and "I am old and used." This allows the students to become more in touch with the item and some of their projections that come up. What they choose to say at times can be profound self descriptions; (b) Do the same exercise but have them choose an animal they would like to be, and make I statements for that. Statements like "I am a squirrel," and "I'm quick" are likely to occur. Ask students what part of the projection was the object and what part did they feel was them.

5. An exercise before rock climbing or some other emotionally and physically strenuous activity is to have each student think of three things they can't do. Have them report one to the group. Have each student change the word "can't" to "won't" and repeat it to the group. Discuss how students felt saying "won't", and owning their shortcomings.

6. *Bitch Session*—This activity can be used at the first sign of tension within the group. It promotes constructive discharge and dealing with the problem. The session needs to be structured well. A student with a bitch expresses it as a resentment to the specific person or the whole group. The student then states his/her demand of that person. This is where the student with the resentment can tell the other person exactly what he/she wants from them to help extinguish the problem. When the demand is through, the student shares an appreciation with the person, similar to the resentment. Example—"Randy, I resent you cooking every meal. I demand that you give someone else a chance and demand that you try some different jobs. I appreciate that you take the initiative every night to start cooking, and I appreciate that you are a good cook."

7. *Fantasy of Getting in Touch with Fear*—This activity is good to use before rock climbing, the ropes course, canoeing, or kayaking. Have students relax with eyes closed. "Take a deep breath and let it all out. Now do this again. Take a trip in your body and find where your fear is located. How big is it? What shape does it have? OK, now breathe through that spot. Get some deep breaths right through that spot. When you're ready open up your eyes." Have them share on a 1–10 point basis what their fear was before and after they focused on it.

8. *Wall Fantasy*—This is best to use directly before rock climbing, solo, or the wall initiative. Tell students you're going to take them on a guided fantasy and at a certain point they are to complete it themselves. Have everybody get in a comfortable spot and close their eyes and relax. Use as many details as possible to provide them with a good representation. Here is an example of a scenario that you might use: "Imagine yourself in a big field. It is very open and it's warm outside. How does the sun feel on your shoulders?" You can feel the grass on your legs. There are some flowers; what colors do you see? On your right is a footpath. You walk over to it and follow it. You walk up a rise and in front of you, you see a wall. Walk up to this wall and complete the fantasy on your own from here. Don't censor, but let whatever comes into your mind come."

When students have finished the fantasy have them share their visualizations in small groups. In the large group explain that the wall can signify a block, challenge, risk, or problem, like they're going to have while rock climbing or on solo. The students created their own wall, the size and what it was made of. Some will have huge walls and some small. Some students will make it over easily, while others won't even try. It is important to share with them how this is their own creation, how they put up their own blocks and created their own difficulties. It's also interesting to see what students have created on the other side of the wall, or their reward. Let the students get whatever they can from this, without you interpreting it for them.

9. *Bragging*—Arrange students in groups of three. Have them pick one quality they do well. Then have them brag about how great they are at it.
   Sabotage—Now with the same quality, have each person in the group tell how and in what way they use it not to believe in themselves.

10. *Alter Ego*—While in group discussions a student may have difficulty expressing his or her feelings. You or another student can go behind him or her and put your hands on his/her shoulders. Then, say what you experience they are feeling as succinctly as possible using "I" statements. If it fits for the student, have them say it. This exercise helps students identify their feelings more and speak from the heart.

Experimentation and Transfer

The following activities are presented to encourage students to experiment with new behaviors. One of the keys in this stage of the group is to have the support and encouragement of the group to try out these new behaviors, without the fear of ridicule or criticism. The atmosphere you want is that of a safe laboratory where failure is impossible and constructive learning is guaranteed.

Role-playing is a good technique for promoting generalization and transfer. Role-playing is used to portray another person or for exploring a different side of one's self. It is best, when used in the middle or end of the course, when the trust level is high. Role-playing can be a high risk activity and some students are more comfortable with it than others. The purpose and objective of the experimentation and transfer exercises are to: (a) allow students to experiment with new behaviors and receive support and constructive feedback; (b) discover what are the ingredients necessary to encourage risk taking; (c) allow students to see how others perceive them; (d) allow students to become more aware of different sides of themselves; (e) allow students to have a clearer perception and practice of their re-entry back home; and, (f) help transfer what has been learned on the adventure-based experience to the home, school, and work setting. Ways in which you can facilitate for experimentation and transfer are:

1. Hold a discussion about the ingredients the group would need from each other to guarantee that it would be a safe laboratory for all to take the risks necessary to be "peak performers."

2. Discuss the type of comments from others that would sabotage or inhibit taking emotional risks.

3. Have each person make a verbal commitment that they will provide a safe environment for others to experiment with new behaviors.

4. Have each person pick a pattern that they are willing to experiment with a behavior change and share what their plan is with the group, i.e., "I will speak up more and offer my ideas" or "I will give others a chance to lead and work on being able to follow today." Ask each person how the group can "help or support you in taking this risk."

5. At the end of the day in your group, ask each member how experimenting with the new behavior went. Get feedback from others and refine what worked and didn't work. Recommit to do it again or try a new behavior.

6. Develop support partners who can coach and support each other on behavior changes. This will help to diversify the type of processing groups you hold. You may want to consider creative matching of your pairs. For example, a leader who wants to be less of one with a passive person who wants to be more assertive. You can have them teach the other person how to do it. A passive person teaching another how to be passive can no longer be unconscious with this process.

7. In the bigger group discuss how individuals can give and receive good coaching on the course and back at school, work, or home. How can you guarantee your coach will be successful?

8. Hold a discussion on sub-personalities, subselves, different sides of a person, or the different voices or conversations we hear inside our heads. Have students be aware of the fact that we all have different sides and that it is normal. The conversations may not go away, but we can get better at managing them.

9. *Fantasy of Subpersonalities*—Have students relaxed with their eyes closed. The setting is in a field. Give many details including that they see some woods in front of them. They walk up to the trees and find a footpath. It leads to a cabin in the woods. Have students fantasize how big is the cabin? "What is it made of?" "What kind of windows does it have?" They walk up to the door. "What does the door look like?" Inside the cabin are all their subpersonalities or different sides of themselves. When they open the door all their subpersonalities are going to come out. Ask them to identify these subpersonalities and say what they want to them. When the students have finished their fantasies have them share them in small groups.

When back together as a large group anyone can share their fantasy with the entire group. This exercise is very effective before the students go on solo. It allows them to become more aware of themselves and their internal voices that they will invariably hear when by themselves.

10. *Role Play Each Member of the Crew*—split up into two groups, and pick half the people to role-play. Set up a scene such as dinner time, breaking camp, or group discussion, and have each group role play the same scene portraying the characters that they have selected. In order to role-play the whole group, this process has to be completed twice. In the role-play, try to capture the characters' body posture, mannerisms, voice, and what that person would say. One group does their role play and then the other group performs theirs. When this has terminated the people playing the same parts, as there should be two of every character, share how they felt playing that role. Ask "What was hard or easy for you?" In the large group, have the two people share what they found about that role, and person, and then have the person they portrayed give their impression of how it was to watch himself or herself, as others perceived them. The role play is also very effective if done before solo.

11. *Re-Entry Role-play*—Have students describe a situation that they are going back to, such as, school, parents, work, or relationships, that is causing them some anxiety. The person whose role-play it is can describe each of the people, their role, and the scene. This person can also play many of the characters. The switching of roles allows the other players to get more of a flavor of the character.

12. *Coaching*—In small groups of two or three, have students pick a behavior or situation they want to change at work or home. Each person can receive coaching from group members about the situation and strategize ways to deal with it at home or work. Have them develop a list of strengths or supports they have or will need along with a plan to counteract the negative forces. This small group can support each other on the new behaviors when the course is over, by deciding to write letters, make phone calls, or arrange meetings. Each member can share their plan back in the big group and receive more feedback. Here they can role-play situations, that will need more practice.

13. *Visualization*—Using their visualization skills have students go back and experience the successes of the course. What did they see? The environment, people's faces, etc. What did they hear from others or nature? How did it feel and where did they feel it? Is there a metaphor that goes with it, an object or a special word? How can they carry this feeling, visualization, and metaphor with them when they get to a new edge?

14. *Anchoring*—When students feel the feelings, hear the positive words and sounds, and see the successful sights and they are all at their peaks, have them touch their hands in a unique way to "anchor" or associate these sensations to this touch. For example, hold their little finger with the fingers of their other hand or make the "OK" sign but use a different finger. Each time they visualize their success, have them hold their anchor until holding their anchor will be conditioned to bring up their successful experiences. Students can then use their anchor when they are in a new or uncomfortable situations as a positive resource. In addition, students can anchor many positive emotional states for future use.

15. Have students use their positive visualization of past successes and their anchor as a preconditioning to visualizing the situation at home, school, or work that they are committed to changing. Then have them visualize the new situation and doing it perfectly and handling any of the issues that may come up. Have them continue to replay the future scene over and over until the results are exactly like they want it.

Keynotes and Cautions

You cannot teach humans anything. You can only help them discover it within themselves.

Galileo

1. Students are the best authorities on themselves. All we can do is bring things to their awareness.

2. Let students know that they can pass on participation in an exercise. It's their responsibility to make their own decisions.

3. Stay with what, how, and where questions. Why's tend to receive rationalizations and lose focus on the experience.

4. There is no need to force these activities. Stay with the concerns of your students. Use these activities only where they fit.

5. Use exercises that you feel comfortable with and do it in your own style.

6. It is a good idea to let students lead some of the activities.

7. Use levity and humor where you can.

Closing Comments

Adventure-based programming is an exciting field to work in. At the same time, learning to be an effective instructor and facilitator is an on-going challenge. Many adventure-based programs spend a significant amount of time doing activities during staff training such as paddling, hiking, sailing, first-aid simulations and reviewing program policies. Frequently, little time is spent discussing strategies and techniques for processing the experience and methods for facilitating the generalization and transfer of insights and skills learned on the adventure course to the participant's life at home.

The potential shortcoming of this approach to staff development was pointed out by Rhoades (1972) who stated "To merely provide an experience, albeit a powerful one, and to expect the student to return home and to sort it out for himself is, . . . to invite failure" (p 104). Similarly, recent research reported by Baldwin, Wagner and Roland (1991) suggests that it is not the experience itself that is the change agent, but rather, it is the knowledge and skills of the facilitator that has a significant impact on program outcomes.

Therefore, as an adventure-based instructor, you have a responsibility to develop a variety of tools that you can use to encourage the growth of individuals and groups. In this text we have provided you with information that is both theoretical and practical in nature. Our goal was to offer you a foundation of resources from which you can draw-on to refine or expand your processing skills. We know that the skills necessary to process the experience are complex and at times challenging to implement. We suggest that processing is an artful science, with training required in scientific skills such as observation of events and behavior, decision making, and refined communicative/interactive skills, such as active listening and giving feedback. Simultaneously, it is a form of art, in that, we cannot follow a planned recipe. What worked with one group may not work with another group. As a result, we need to be flexible and trust our knowledge, skills, and intuition. We need to be able to recognize what is happening in the group and take the risk to ask a question, do an activity, or make a statement that feels right at that moment.

As a facilitator and instructor, you play an essential role in the lives of the students that you interact with. We encourage you to set personal goals and seek to increase your knowledge and skills. If you approach the development of skills for effectively processing the experience in a manner similar to the way that you learn to master the skills to become a seasoned sailor, paddler, mountaineer, counselor, teacher, or skier, then, you and your students will grow and benefit from your ability to design and deliver a quality educational and/or therapeutic adventure-based experiences.

Our answer, must consist, not in talk and meditation, but in right action and in right conduct. Life ultimately means taking responsibility to find the right answer to its problems and to fulfill the tasks which it constantly sets for each individual.

—Viktor E. Frankl
Man's Search for Meaning

References and Suggested Reading List

Alexander, F., & French, T. (1946). *Psychoanalytic therapy*. New York: Ronald Press Co.

Bacon, S. (1983). *The conscious use of metaphor in Outward Bound*. Denver, CO: Colorado Outward Bound School.

Bagby, S. A., & Chavarria, L. S. (1980). Important issues in outdoor education: ERIC/Cress Mini Review. *Outdoor Adventure Education and Juvenile Delinquents*. (ERIC Document Reproduction Service No. ED 191 639).

Baldwin, T. T., Wagner, R. J., & Roland, C. C. (1991). *Effects of outdoor challenge training on group and individual perceptions*. Manuscript submitted for publication.

Barker, J. (1985). *Discovering the future: A necessary unity*. New York: Dutton.

Bateson, G. (1979). *Mind and nature: A necessary unity*. New York: Dutton.

Beck, A. T. (1979). *Cognitive therapy and emotional disorders*. New York: New American Library.

Brown, G. I. (1971). *Human teaching for human learning: An introduction to confluent education*. New York: Viking Press.

Brown, G. I., Yeoman, T., & Grizzard, T. (1975). *The live classroom: Innovation through confluent education and gestalt*. New York: Viking Press.

Bruner, E. (1988). Experience and its expressions. In V. Turner & E. Bruner (Eds.), *The anthropology of experience*. Chicago: University of Illinois Press.

Bruner, J. (1962). *On knowing: Essays for the left hand*. Cambridge, MA: Belknap Press of Harvard University.

Buller, P. F., Cragun, J. R., McEvoy, G. M. (1991). Getting the most out of outdoor training. *Training & Development Journal, 45*(3), 58–61.

Burns, D. (1980). *Feeling good: The new mood therapy*. New York: William Morrow and Co.

Capra, F. (1986). Paradigms and paradigm shifts. *ReVision, 9*(1), 11.

Carkhoff, R. R., Pierce, R. H., & Cannon, J. R. (1980). *The art of helping*. Amherst, MA: Human Resource Development Press, Inc.

Castillo, G. (1974). *Left-handed teaching—Lessons in affective education*. New York: Praeger Publishing.

Cohen, A., & Smith, R. (1976). *The critical incident in growth groups: Theory and practice*. La Jolla, CA: University and Associates.

Colan, N. (1986). *Outward Bound: An annotated bibliography 1976–1985*. Connecticut: Outward Bound.

Combs, G., & Freedman, J. (1990). *Symbol, story and ceremony: Using metaphor in individual and family therapy*. New York: W. W. Norton & Co.

Corey, M. S., & Corey, G. (1987). *Groups: Process and practice*. Belmont, CA: Brooks/Cole Publishing Co.

Dewey, J. (1938). *Experience and education*. New York: Collier Books.

Dyer, W. G. (1972). An inventory of trainer interventions. In R. C. Diedrick & H. A. Dye (Eds.), *Group procedures: Purpose, processes, and outcomes* (pp. 115–119). Boston: Houghton Mifflin.

Ebbe, C. (1985). *Group leadership and techniques*. Unpublished manuscript.

Egan, G. (1986). *The skilled helper: A systematic approach to effective helping*. Monterey, CA: Brooks/Cole.

Ellis, A. (1975). *A new guide to rational living.* North Hollywood, CA: Wilshire Books.

Erickson, M.H. (1948/1980). *Hypnotic psychotherapy.* In E. L. Rossi (Ed.), *The collected papers of Milton H. Erickson on hypnosis. Vol. IV. Innovative hypnotherapy.* New York: Irvington.

Ewert, A. W. (1989). *Outdoor adventure pursuits: Foundations, models, and theories.* Columbus, Ohio: Publishing Horizons, Inc.

Fabian, K. J. (1984). *Directed affective treatment.* Unpublished manuscript.

Fabian, K. J., Edelhofer, F. E., & Edelhofer, S. F. (1985). *Directed affective treatment: A step beyond empathy.* Unpublished manuscript.

Gass, M. A. (1985). Programming the transfer of learning in adventure activities. *The Journal of Experiential Education, 8*(3), 18–24.

Gazda, G. M., Asbury, F. S., Balzer, F. J., Childres, W. C., & Walters, R. P. (1984). *Human relations development: A manual for educators.* Newton, MA: Allyn and Bacon, Inc.

Gerstein, J. (1988). *The human side of adventure challenge.* Unpublished manuscript.

Grove, D. J. (1989). *Resolving feelings of anger, guilt and shame.* Edwardsville, IL: David Grove Seminars.

Hagberg, J., & Leider, R. (1982). *The inventurers: Excursions in life and career renewal.* Menlo Park, CA: Addison-Wesley Publishing, Inc.

Haley, J. (1973). *Uncommon therapy: The psychiatric techniques of Milton H. Erickson, M.D.* New York: W. W. Norton & Co.

Heider, J. (1985). *The tao of leadership: Leadership strategies for a new age.* New York: Bantam Books.

Humphrey, L. L., & Stern, S. (1988). Object relation and the family system in bulimia: A theoretical integration. *Journal of Marital and Family Therapy, 14*(4), 337–350.

Jacobs, E. E., Harvill, R. L., & Masson, R. L. (1988). *Group counseling: Strategies and skills.* Belmont, CA: Brooks/Cole Publishing Co.

Jeffers, S. (1987). *Feel the fear and do it anyway.* New York: Ballantine Books.

Kalisch, K. R. (1979). *The role of the instructor in the Outward Bound educational process.* Three Lakes, WI: Honey Rock Camp.

Knapp, C. E. (1984). Designing processing questions to meet specific objectives. *The Journal of Experiential Education, 7*(2), 47–49.

Kolb, D. A. (1984). *Experiential learning: Experience as the source of learning and development.* Englewood Cliffs, NJ: Prentice-Hall, Inc.

Korzybski, A. (1951). The role of language in perceptual processes. In R. Blake & G. Ramsey (Eds.), *Perception: An approach to personality.* New York: Ronald Press.

Kuhn, T. (1962). *The structure of scientific revolutions.* Chicago: University of Chicago Press.

Langer, S. K. (1948). *Philosophy in a new key: A study of the symbolism of reason, rite, and art.* New York: Mentor.

Lononcy, L. (1977). *The motivating leader.* New York: Prentice-Hall, Inc.

Mahoney, M. J. (1982). Psychotherapy and human change processes. In *The master lecture series: Vol. I. Psychotherapy resource and behavior change.* Washington D.C.: American Psychological Association.

Merritt, R. E., & Walley, D. D. (1977). *The group leader's handbook: Resources, techniques and survival skills.* Champaign, IL: Research Press Co.

Nadler, G. & Hibino S. (1990). *Breakthrough thinking.* Rocklin, California: Prima Publishing & Communications.

Nadler, R. S. (1977). *Instructors guide to confluent education curriculum: Outdoor adventure programs.* Unpublished manuscript.

Nemeth, M. (1990). *You and money seminar.* University of California, Santa Barbara Extension. March and April.

North Carolina Outward Bound School. (1980). *Instructor's field manual.* Author.

Norton, C.A.C. (1978). *Effects of training in detection and use of nonverbal behavior on counselor effectiveness.* Unpublished doctoral dissertation, University of Northern Colorado.

O'Hanlon, W. H. (1990). A grand unified theory for brief therapy: Putting problems in context. In J. K. Zeig & S. G. Gilligan (Eds.), *Brief therapy: Myths, methods, and metaphors.* New York: Banner/Mazel Publishers.

The Oxford dictionary of current English. (1990). New York: Oxford University Press.

Pascale, R. T. (1990). *Managing on the edge.* New York: Simon and Schuster.

Perls, F. S. (1969). *Gestalt therapy verbatim.* Moab, Utah: Real People Press.

Peters, T. (1987). *Thriving on chaos.* New York: Harper & Row Publishing.

Piaget, J. (1954). *The construction of reality in the child.* New York: Basic Books.

Piaget, J. (1977). Equilibration processes in the psychobiological development of the child. In H. E. Gruber & J. J. Voneche (Eds.), *The essential Piaget.* New York: Basic Books.

Prigogine, I., & Steagers, I. (1984). *Order out of chaos! Man's new dialogue with nature.* New York: Bantom.

Quinsland, L. K., & Van Ginkel, A. (1984). How to process experience. *The Journal of Experiential Education, 7*(2), 8–13.

Rhoades, J. S. (1972). *The problem of individual change in Outward Bound: An application of change and transfer theory.* Unpublished doctoral dissertation, University of Massachusetts.

Robbins, A. (1980). *Unlimited power.* New York: Ballantine Books.

Rudolph, S. (1991). *A naturalistic investigation of the therapeutic effects of an adventure-based family enrichment and interventions program.* Unpublished doctoral dissertation, Northern Illinois University.

Rycroft, C. (1979). *The innocence of dreams: A new approach to the study of dreams.* New York: Pantheon Press.

Schoel, J., Prouty, D., & Radcliffe, P. (1988). *Islands of healing: A guide to adventure based counseling.* Hamilton, MA: Project Adventure, Inc.

Siegelman, E. Y. (1990). *Metaphor and meaning in psychotherapy.* New York: The Guilford Press.

Simon, S. F., Howe, L. W., & Kirshenbaum, R. (1972). *Values clarification—A handbook of practical strategies for teachers and students.* New York: Hart Publishing Co.

Smith, K. (1984). Rabbits, lynxes, and organizational transitions. In J. Kimberly & R. Quinn, (Eds.), *Managing organizational transitions.* Homewood, IL: Irwin.

Thompson, S. C. (1981). Will it hurt less if I can control it? A complex answer to a simple question. *Psychological Bulletin, 90,* 84–101.

Tomm, K. (1988). Interventive interviewing, Part 3: Intending to ask lineal, circular, strategic, or reflexive questions? *Family Process, 27*(1), 1–15.

Tracy, B. (1987). *Psychology of achievement.* Chicago, IL: Nightingale-Conant Corporation.

Trudeau, K. (1989). *Mega memory.* New York: American Memory Institute.

Viscott, D. (1976). *The language of feelings.* New York: Simon and Schuster, Inc.

Voyageur Outward Bound School (1988). *Instructor handbook.* Minnetonka, MN: Author.

Wagner, R. J., Baldwin, T. T., & Roland, C. C. (1991). Outdoor training: Revolution or fad? *Training & Development Journal, 45*(3), 51–56.

Walsh, V., & Golins, G. (1976). *The exploration of the Outward Bound process.* Unpublished manuscript, Denver, CO.

Watzlawick, P. (1990, July & August). *Brief strategic therapy,* paper presented at the Mental Research Institute, Palo Alto, California.

Watzlawick, P. (1987). If you desire to see, learn how to act. In J. K. Zeig (Ed.), *Evolution of psychotherapy.* New York: Bruner/Mazel Publishers.

Wegscheider, S. (1979). *The family trap. . . .: No one escapes from a chemically dependent family.* St. Paul, MN: Nurturing Network.

Weinstein, G., Hardin, J., & Weinstein, M. (1970). *Education of the self: A trainer's manual.* Amherst, MA: Mandala Press.

Wheeles, A. (1973). *How people change.* New York: Harper and Row Books.

White, M., & Epston, D. (1990). *Narrative means to therapeutic ends.* New York: W. W. Norton & Co.

Winnicott, D. W. (1965). *The maturational process and the facilitating environment.* New York: International Universities Press.

Yalom, I. D. (1985). *The theory and practice of group psychotherapy.* New York: Basic Books.

Zinker, J. (1977). *Creative process in gestalt therapy.* New York: Random House.